MEDITATIONS
for
MOMS-TO-BE

MEDITATIONS
for
MOMS-TO-BE

SANDRA DRESCHER-LEHMAN

Good Books

Intercourse, PA 17534

Acknowledgments

Scripture quotations from The New Revised Standard Version of the Bible. Copyright ©1989 by the Division of Christian Education of The National Council of the Churches of Christ in the USA. Used by permission. All rights reserved.

Cover design and art by Cheryl Benner
Design by Dawn J. Ranck

MEDITATIONS FOR MOMS-TO-BE
© 1995 by Good Books, Intercourse, PA 17534
International Standard Book Number: 1-56148-182-3
Library of Congress Catalog Card Number: 95-36210

Library of Congress Cataloging-in-Publication Data

Drescher-Lehman, Sandra.
    Meditations for moms-to-be / Sandra Drescher-Lehman.
        p. cm.
    ISBN 1-56148-182-3
    1. Mothers--Prayer-books and devotions--English.
2. Pregnant women--Prayer-books and devotions--English.
3. Motherhood--Religious aspects--Christianity--Meditations. I. Title.
BV4847.D738 1995
242'.6431--dc20   95-36210
                                    CIP

To my mother and mother-in-law,
Betty Drescher and Louisa Lehman,
whose second and fifth pregnancies
enabled my own,
and whose love continues to enrich me.

About This Book

Nothing can compare to the exhilaration and panic that entered my soul simultaneously each time I discovered that a baby was alive within me! I was overwhelmed by the thought that this barely perceptible life would one day call me "Mom."

My desire that no one should experience this miraculous time of life as a time of loneliness led me to put my own thoughts and feelings into words to share with other Moms-to-Be.

May these brief commentaries, ideas, and scriptures offer you companionship and permission to be honest as you live through the ups and downs of pregnancy. May these thoughts be a gift to you as you put wordless energy into giving to your baby. May they lead to a deeper awareness of being loved by your Creator and Eternal Parent.

—*Sandra Drescher-Lehman*

Joy

I've always wanted to be pregnant. In my tenth grade biology class I developed the sensation of having a baby inside me when I read about how a baby grows within a female body. The miracle of how two people can create an embryo, which grows into a fetus, which is already a tiny person, astounds me. To believe that all that is happening inside me right now is almost too amazing! I wonder. Can it really be true?

I was never too sure what I would do with a baby after the pregnant part was over. I guess as I live out this time of preparation, I'll figure that out, too.

**Thank you, God,
for the miracle of your continuing creation.**

---

*May you be blessed by the Lord,
who made heaven and earth.*
Psalm 115:15

Busy Without Motion

The urgency of today's duties vanished with my first waking thought. I'm pregnant again today! It's like the first warm day of spring, when every plan gives way to the impulse to soak in the sun. It's as if I myself am a growing bulb. The same feeling comes with the first big snow of winter, when the whole world lies bound in an awesome hush.

That's how it is today, only better. It's the day after my wonderful discovery. My world stops to receive this gift. My imagination watches how busily my inner body works to prepare a new space. My future has been forever altered. I can tell that I won't have time to do anything else today.

Take time to marvel.

Then Mary said, "Here am I, the servant of the Lord;
let it be with me according to your word." . . .
Luke 1:38

Beyond Head and Heart

*J*f it were up to my head, this baby would never be born! I have no experience with that. Even if I did, I'd still have no idea how to begin to give birthing instructions to my body.

If it were up to my heart, this baby would never get past cell one, either. I'm so enthralled with the idea of being pregnant, that I'm not worth anything on the production end of things.

I'm thankful that most of the work of growing this baby is not up to me! A few baby manuals and baby experts exist, but most of the work of creation will happen despite what I know to do and feel. I call this a miracle of pure love.

Surrender yourself to this love.

Above all, clothe yourselves with love,
which binds everything together in perfect harmony.
Colossians 3:14

How Soon Can I Tell?

One minute I feel like shouting the news for the whole world to hear — I'M PREGNANT! Then, before I do, I'm not sure I want to tell anyone at all. It's too special to say aloud. I'll just treasure the secret inside for a while.

My sister never told anyone when she was pregnant until after the first trimester. But I don't think I can wait that long. I think I'll just tell one person . . . well, maybe two . . . or five!

**Give thanks
to your Creator.**

Sing to the Lord with thanksgiving . . .
Psalm 147:7

My Timing

everyone's different. That gives me permission to not follow my sister's example about when to announce my pregnancy. She hesitated to tell people too early because miscarriages are more likely to happen in the first trimester. But if I do have a miscarriage, I'll want people to know so they can feel sad with me—at least my good friends. For me, sharing doubles my joy and helps me bear my sadness.

I think I just talked myself into making a formal announcement. I'll start by telling every friend I see.

**Know that whenever you choose
to tell the news,
it is the right time.**

. . . a time to keep silence, and a time to speak.
Ecclesiastes 3:7

Infertile

I was beginning to think I'd never get pregnant. The longer we tried without success, the more pessimistic I became. I thought maybe I should start adjusting to the idea of not having children.

My longing to be a mother, however, grew stronger because of the wait. Every month my hopes built until that fateful first sign of bleeding. Every month, the crash felt harder; tears sneaked closer to the surface. Some days I skipped the pain and simply got angry. Why couldn't I be a mother?

Now I *am* going to be a mother! Tears and joy—and memories of waiting—blend to keep me from taking this miracle for granted.

**Remember, today,
the women
who long to be mothers.**

*[The Lord] gives the barren woman a home,
making her the joyous mother of children.
Praise the Lord!*
Psalm 113:9

Nine Months Is Too Long!

As soon as I told my sister that I might be pregnant, she got a pin for me to wear that says, "Due in January." January seems so far away! How will I ever be able to wait that long?

I want to know who this child looks like. I want to count her fingers and toes. I want to see what color eyes and hair he has. Or is she bald? (I hope not.)

Will I be able to love someone I haven't met yet? I can hardly wait to play with him and read to her. This is harder than waiting for Christmas when I was a kid!

**Spend your anticipating energy
on preparing
one thing for your baby.**

---

*Commit your way to the Lord;
trust in him, and he will act.*
Psalm 37:5

Nine Months Is Not So Long!

*Y*esterday I wondered how in the world I could wait nine months to meet my baby face-to-face. Today I can't imagine how I'll ever get everything done before the baby comes!

Besides all the usual busyness of my life, I now have to prepare a whole new place in my home to protect a child. I have to prepare attitudes within me to nurture a baby. I have to prepare a new mindset that will welcome a person to forever be a part of my life.

Nine months is not so long after all. I don't know who needs this incubation time the most—my baby or me!

**Start a journal
to keep a record
of the feelings and activities
of your pregnancy.**

---

*. . . my covenant of peace
shall not be removed,
says the Lord.*
Isaiah 54:10

Stability

I've taken some secret pride in my many moves as an adult. Since leaving home, I've lived in 16 different places. I've entertained myself by using the unique aspects of each setting to create a home. Stability seems to come from within me, rather than from my surroundings.

I wonder if I've been able to delight in these transitions—even grow and blossom through them—because of stability in my childhood home. We lived in the same old farm house for 18 years. Now that I'm pregnant, I'm suddenly thinking bigger than myself, beyond what I need and enjoy. Maybe it's time to consider what my child needs to be rooted for life.

Think about what home will mean for your child.

Because the Lord your God
travels along with your camp,
. . . your camp must be holy . . .
Deuteronomy 23:14

13

Eating Words

At one point in my life I said I was never going to have children. That's what working with incarcerated women and children for 10 years did for me! Why would I invite that kind of trouble and heartache?

I was never going to get married, either. I was a staunch and proud single woman . . . until I met John. Those were sweet words to eat!

It's time to eat my words again. It's funny; I don't mind it this time, either.

**Life is too short
to be rigid.**

---

*[The Lord] put a new song
in my mouth . . .*
Psalm 40:3

Light to the World

Why would I want to bring someone else into this world? It's already over-populated and full of famine and violence. Could I really be thinking of the well-being of another human soul and still allow life and birth to happen?

Those questions from friends, and from within myself, kept me from wanting to have children for a long time. But then another thought grew within me. Maybe my child will relieve some of the world's suffering. My child could be a bright spot of love and joy. The world can always use more of that. Peacefulness may be embodied in the person my child grows into.

Of course I want to bring a baby into this world.

**Imagine a glow of love,
filling and surrounding your baby,
even now.**

*. . . Your children
will be like olive shoots
around your table.*
Psalm 128:3

Selfish?

While I've always had friends warning me against adding to the world's population, I've also had voices asking if selfishness was keeping me from having children. Neither side had the final influence, though.

My decisive moment came at a family gathering. While watching my parents' joy as they interacted with their children, in-laws, and grandchildren, I knew I wanted to have that kind of fun in my home at that age, too.

Of course, children will be a lot of work. And they will also bring a lot of joy.

**Imagine yourself
as a grandma!**

*May you see your children's
children . . .*
Psalm 128:6

Due Date

I don't know how many times in the past I flipped the pages on my calendar to see when the due date would be if I were pregnant this month. Now, at last, I am pregnant, and the due date is always the same. I still flip, though, just to be sure. Sure of what, I don't know. Maybe I need to continually validate that this truly is happening to me! The due date is real this time, and it only comes closer each time I count.

Oh, joy. What a miracle! Pregnancy is what I will live for the next nine months!

**Decorate your due date
on the calendar!**

---

*May the glory of the Lord
endure forever;
may the Lord rejoice in his works.*
Psalm 104:31

Naps

T hank goodness, I have a husband who thinks naps are valuable. I need someone to encourage me when I feel like I wasted a valuable afternoon off from work by sleeping. It's not something I ever let slip into my schedule before; my brain is having a hard time believing it's necessary.

Necessary or not, I simply can't stay awake. My body has taken over the decision-making process for my intellect again today. So when John came home and asked what I did with my free afternoon, I told him that what I mostly did was take a nap.

His reply was comforting. "Good job, Sandy," he said.

**Be assured
that by napping
you are loving both yourself
and your baby.**

---

*I lie down and sleep;
I wake again,
for the Lord sustains me.*
Psalm 3:5

Exhaustion

Remembering yesterday afternoon's nap and the encouragement I received for having taken it, I'm not sure how I will make it at my desk until five o'clock today. I've never heard of anyone needing to quit their job because they were one month pregnant and constantly tired, but I'm thinking there's a first time for everything!

By two o'clock I am so tired that I eat a chocolate candy bar to pep me up. It does . . . for half an hour. Then I plummet to a weariness that puts me to sleep in the lounge during my next break! I think I'm going to have to try something different tomorrow.

**Eliminate the evening's
nonessential activities.**

---

*. . . Give light to my eyes,
or I will sleep
the sleep of death.*
Psalm 13:3

Creative Fatigue

For my morning "meditation," I was reading about the first month of pregnancy. That's the only time of day I'm awake enough to read! The information is helpful because now I know why I'm so tired. My body's building the placenta to support my baby's life, besides adjusting to the emotional and physical changes that come with pregnancy.

The bad news: the fatigue will last three months. At least I know what's going on, though. It helps to think about the busy factory of machinery working inside me. Today I'll take a walk with that image in my head, skip the candy bar, and go to bed early tonight.

**When you can't take the longed-for nap,
stay busy in a gentle sort of way.**

Sweet is the sleep of laborers . . .
Ecclesiastes 5:12

Doubts

What if I'm not really pregnant? Wouldn't that be a sad joke? How reliable are tests, anyway? I do feel lots of pregnancy symptoms. My body is definitely preparing itself to carry a baby. But what if the doctors are wrong? Am I capable of making up something this big?

I should try to not be so excited yet. I can't seem to help it, though. I have to be pregnant. I'm sure I'm pregnant. Well, almost . . .

**Let God ride the other end
of your emotional see-saw.**

*May my meditation be pleasing to him,
for I rejoice in the Lord.*
Psalm 104:34

In Sickness . . .

I've been trying so hard to eat right and get lots of sleep and remember to take my vitamins, and now it feels like I'm coming down with another cold! It's only been two weeks since I recovered from the last one, which zapped my energy and patience for a month before that. Maybe this baby is wreaking more havoc on my body than I know. It's certainly his fault that I'm left to recover without any medication.

Is this merely a foretaste of what this child will bring to my life—more germs, little resistance, and far less sleep than ever? Pregnant women should have to repeat some version of their marriage vows to each child they bear: For better or worse, in sickness and in health. Or maybe we should make the vows *before* the birth.

**Lord, help me to deal with
and appreciate whatever this child brings to me.**

---

*Let your father and mother be glad;
let her who bore you rejoice.*
Proverbs 23:25

Forgetting the Past

I'm wearing out quickly from reading about all the possible hazards to a baby—microwave rays, air pollution, sweeteners, toxic chemicals in cleaning fluids and water, second-hand smoke, drugs. I think I've already made some mistakes before I knew I was pregnant. This is a risky adventure I've just begun. But I can't be consumed by the hazards.

My grandmother didn't have to worry about all those things! On the other hand, in spite of all the warnings, there's been no safer time in history to be pregnant and give birth. I'm glad to be alive now and glad to be giving life to another now.

**Forget mistakes you've already made,
and start now to make
the best decisions possible.**

*. . . this one thing I do:
forgetting what lies behind
and straining forward to what lies ahead,
I press on toward the goal for the prize
of the heavenly call of God in Christ Jesus.*
Philippians 3:13,14

Wrapped in Light

$\mathcal{L}$ast night I wakened without opening my eyes. I felt like everything inside me was illuminating my whole body, lighting up the room, spreading into the whole world. It felt like a dream, but there were no pictures or words—just light. I felt an excited stirring, like I remember having when I was little and woke up on the first day of school. It was anticipation then, tempered with a tinge of fear of the unknown. But I was always eager to get going and find out what was to come.

My brain struggled to find the reason for the light. Where was I? What is today? What time is it?

Then I remembered. I'm pregnant!

**Close your eyes
and imagine your baby projecting light
into your body
and into your life.**

---

*. . . O Lord, my God,
you are very great.
You are clothed with honor and majesty,
wrapped in light as with a garment . . .*
Psalm 104:1,2

Planning

I wish I could turn off the switch in my mind that is continuously, forever, planning. I'm planning each day. I'm planning what has to get done before the baby comes. I'm planning how to handle a miscarriage (just in case). I'm planning how to schedule my life after the baby is born. I'm planning how to be with the baby more—and how to take breaks from the baby!

I've always enjoyed working with details, but the kind of planning my mind keeps trying to click into now feels like wasted time. Most of it will never be needed.

Maybe my subconscious is simply trying to cope with all the unknown changes entering my life with this new discovery. Maybe I need to spend less energy trying to stop my thinking and, instead, let it guide me.

Protect my planning mind, Lord.

Save us, we beseech you, O Lord!
O Lord, we beseech you, give us success!
Psalm 118:25

Attitude

Today this house is oppressive. I feel like an invalid, all curled up in a blanket in the easy chair. The day's so gloomy that I have to turn on a light to read my little books. I just got awake and I'm already tired. I have to eat something, but I'd rather not. The dog is breathing very noisily and it irritates me.

I know someone looking in from the outside would be jealous of me. What a gift to have time to relax, to randomly fall in and out of sleep, to warm a cozy spot on a damp day, to have plenty of food in the refrigerator and a dog for companionship.

I could use an attitude adjustment! I don't have the energy, though, to turn the knob . . .

Remember the gifts of yesterday.

*Awake, put on strength,
O arm of the Lord!
Awake as in days of old . . .*
Isaiah 51:9

Joy

I can still hardly believe there's another person inside me! John and I talked and figured and debated for so long about doing this. When would be a good time to be pregnant? How much money do we need to provide for a baby's needs? The first day of pregnancy suddenly makes those questions obsolete. It's no longer a debate or economic equation. It's a baby!

Maybe God got tired waiting for us to decide when the ideal time was to receive this gift. Now that our baby is on the way, it seems like the perfect time. The whole year is pregnant with anticipation. What a joyful time to be alive.

**List the good things
about the timing of your pregnancy.**

You crown the year with your bounty . . .
Psalm 65:11

New Season

It's an age-old season to many, many people, but for me it's here for the first time. Pregnancy is blooming and bringing me an entirely new awareness of the world.

At yard sales I see the baby things people are selling, instead of their books and furniture. I never knew people had so many stories to tell about children, babies, and pregnancy. I'm now the captive and, usually happy, recipient. Have there always been magazines about mothering lying around in every waiting room in this city?

It feels like I'm waking up to the first snowfall. Others have seen it before, but I just noticed that it covers my entire world. Pregnancy. Babies. Motherhood. It all suddenly and completely fills the air.

**Let yourself be enchanted
by this new season.**

*You have never heard,
you have never known,
from of old your ear has not been opened . . .*
Isaiah 48:8

People told us we should get a pet before we had children so we could see each other in the role of parent. We would also discover what it's like to make room for a dependent in our lives. It was a good idea.

Tipper has helped me re-evaluate my materialistic side. Does it really matter that my favorite pillow is torn to shreds? Of what eternal value is the mint condition of the antique washstand from my grandparents' house?

If I can make allowances for an animal, I have confidence that our home and hearts are big enough to share them with the energies of our child. My one concern now is how our dog will react when he meets the competition!

Thank you, God, for the sort of parental preparation our dog has provided.

. . . It is not fair to take the children's food and throw it to the dogs.
Matthew 15:26

I'm beginning to notice, more and more, inter-action between mothers and their children. Out on the sidewalk I see a mother showing her little boy how to tie his shoes. I pass a mother in the grocery store, helping her daughter learn how to control her desires. I see my friend letting her toddler help make cookies. I watch a first-grader following along in the hymnal as her mother points to the words they're singing. Another mother teaches her son how she can love him, even when she's angry about what he's doing.

I've always been certain that being a teacher is not one of my gifts. It's slowly sinking in, however, that becoming a mother means I'd better start adjusting my sense of who I am. By definition, I will also be a teacher. I have two options: discover how to be a good one, or insist on believing that I'm not a teacher, which I will likely prove by the way I treat my child.

**Don't limit your potential
by your perception of who you are,
and by refusing to learn new skills.**

The Lord God has given me the tongue of a teacher . . .
Isaiah 50:4

Life

The mother of one of my friends died this week. Although my friend is in her 50s and her mother was 89, my friend was not ready for her mother to die yet. My friend lives in Richmond, Virginia, and her mother lived in Winnipeg, Manitoba. They didn't have daily contact, yet each was available to the other by letter or phone or plane, when either one needed or wanted to be in touch. I'm beginning to believe that a mother is never dispensable.

I am also realizing that the length of time that I will have a mother, and the length of time that I will be a mother, is not my choice. I can only pray that I enjoy both sides of the mother-child relationship as fully as possible as long as each lasts.

**Keep me as far as possible, Lord,
from an attitude of taking love and life
for granted.**

*. . . I trust in you, O Lord;
I say, "You are my God."
My times are in your hand . . .*
Psalm 31:14,15

Way of Life

Sometimes I think about how my life will be remembered after I die. I've usually thought in terms of accomplishments. What great things will I have done that will make a difference in the world? How strong a resumé will I have built?

When I think about being a mother, it seems too big, too all-encompassing, to consider it a job. It's more than a job. It's going to be a way of life! I need to think now about my character, my personality. How can I be, for this child, as gentle and loving and forgiving as the One who parents me?

**Read a story from the gospels
about the character of Jesus.**

*Sing praises to the Lord,
O you his faithful ones,
and give thanks to his holy name.
For . . . his favor is for a lifetime . . .*
Psalm 30:4,5

Waiting

Waiting has always seemed to me to be a passive word. I see people waiting for the bus—just sitting there. People in nursing homes wait to die. Waiting is the opposite of doing.

This waiting for a baby to be born, though, is anything but passive. This waiting is packed with the explosion potential of a cold kernel of popcorn. What may look like waiting for a baby to be born is actually me strengthening myself for each new development. Every day takes energy not only to exist, but to move toward who I want to be by the day of birth. I have to be quiet on the outside, sometimes, to give my inner self time to grow.

Maybe other people I see waiting are really living strongly and courageously.

**Write a paragraph in your journal
about what kind of a waiter you are.**

*Be strong,
and let your heart take courage,
all you who wait for the Lord.*
Psalm 31:24

Missing Grandpa

John's dad died two years before we were married. I never got to meet him, and I've always been sad about that. I often wish I could have known him.

Now I feel the grief of not knowing my baby's grandfather even more intensely. He is one person who would have undoubtedly shared our joy and helped us nurture this child through the years. We could have bragged unashamedly to him about his precocious grandchild, and he would have shared our pride. Maybe he would have carried a "Brag Book" of his own, kept well supplied with up-to-date photos.

I miss my father-in-law, whose lap will never hold my child. I miss him for my baby who will never know this grandpa.

Cherish the love that you have received from those who have died, that love which has contributed to your being blessed.

Precious in the sight of the Lord is the death of his faithful ones.
Psalm 116:15

Really Living

When I think about how much I miss my father-in-law, I remember all the people who are still alive who will love my baby. These are the people from whom I can still learn. I can listen to their stories. I can receive their love and give them mine. I won't worry about giving them too many photos of my baby.

These are the friends and relatives who will love this baby. With them I will share the life of my child and our journey together as a growing family.

**Give thanks for your friends and family
who will help you love your baby.**

*I walk before the Lord
in the land of the living.*
Psalm 116:9

35

Chosen Vessel

$\mathcal{I}$t's hard to believe that I have a baby inside me that, in the first month of its life, is no bigger than a grain of rice. It's even harder to believe that in the next couple of weeks its heart, digestive tract, sensory organs, neural tube, and arm and leg buds will begin to form. How can something so tiny be a person and already be so intricately designed?

The element of mystery tingles my brain. This is something so far beyond my imagination and ability to create that I'm almost paralyzed with awe at the thought that I am the chosen vessel.

I can't explain what's happening inside me, but I don't have to. I don't have to understand it to be a useful instrument. I simply am, and I hold my baby.

**Close your eyes
and "watch" God forming the baby
your body holds.**

---

*Then the word of the Lord came to me . . .
Just like the clay in the potter's hand,
so are you in my hand.*
Jeremiah 18:5,6

Greasy Food

I used to love coming home when the air was full of fried onions and peppers. Now I get sick when I smell the neighbors frying something! My heightened sense of smell is incredible. I know this body of mine less and less every day.

I have no idea what to make for supper. Even thinking about it makes me sick. Thinking about someone else making it anywhere near my nose nauseates me.

I have to eat, though, or I'll be sicker than ever in a couple of hours. I guess our "eating out" budget will have to expand again tonight for the sake of this mother-baby duo.

**Let your lifestyle
enjoy the flexibility your body demands.**

---

*. . . do you not know that your body
is a temple of the Holy Spirit within you,
which you have from God,
and that you are not your own?*
I Corinthians 6:19

Competence

For 30 years, I put off the decision about whether or not to have children. At 20 I knew I was too young. At 25, friends my age were becoming parents, but I still had too many other plans for my life. At 30, I wished I had another 15 years to decide. I still felt too young.

Now that we are taking the route of the parenting adventure, I know it will be like many other previous choices. Some days I will feel incompetent, and some days I will know mastery. At least I *hope to* experience the latter every now and then!

**Think about the things
that being pregnant causes you to give up
and what things it adds to your life.**

---

*. . . to set the mind on the Spirit
is life and peace.*
Romans 8:6

I certainly didn't expect the reaction I got today. I told Deb I'm pregnant and she burst into tears! She apologized, saying she wanted to be happy with me, but it was just one more slap in the face, reminding her that she can't get pregnant.

I had been eager to tell Deb because she obviously loves children, and I thought she would be excited with me. I had no idea about the pain in which she's been living. In the middle of my joy, I am jolted to realize how insensitive I've been to the suffering of others.

**Pray for someone you know
who has been unable to have children.**

*[Hannah] was deeply distressed
and prayed to the Lord,
and wept bitterly.*
I Samuel 1:10

My Baby—Also a Grandchild

I never was a wonderful softball player, but I have usually been able to get to first base without falling flat on my face. After last Monday night's game, however, I no longer have even that much assurance. Late in the game, while playing third base, I missed a ball. It hit me in the stomach. I was totally embarrassed. That probably should have convinced me to quit. Instead, I renewed my resolve to not let my pregnancy deny me the basic enjoyments of summer life. Besides, I'm not that far along.

Today I got a letter from my mother who lives two hours away, telling me I better give up softball for the sake of her grandchild! How did she find out? That was one thing I had decided not to tell her. My life is not mine!

**You are not alone in your pregnancy—
for better or for worse!**

---

*By the tender mercy of our God,
the dawn from on high will break upon us.*
Luke 1:78

Changing Roles

stayed up late last night, making my husband a Father's Day card. I don't think he was quite ready for this unexpected push into his new identity. Maybe I put a lot of time into the card as a way of coping with my own adjustment to this change.

Eight years ago I chose to marry a friend whom I knew would make a good father, but we don't know each other as parents yet. He's a fun uncle, but I don't know him as Daddy. He doesn't know me as Mother, either. We don't know ourselves as parents!

**Lord, help our marital love expand
with the size of our family.**

. . . This is my beloved and this is my friend . . .
Song of Solomon 5:16

Coffee

I thought coffee would be one of the hardest things to give up when I was considering pregnancy. I started drinking it when I was 16 because it didn't have any calories, and I wanted to lose weight. I learned to love it, both for its taste and the fun of drinking something hot. It's the incentive I need, sometimes, when I'm having a hard time crawling out of bed in the morning. It's a cozy sort of pleasure to hold and sip when I'm with friends. The varieties without caffeine have just never held the same zip and depth of taste for me.

My worst fears about how I would give it up, however, are all beside the point. I don't have to struggle with the temptation about whether or not to drink it while I'm pregnant, because I can't even smell it these days without feeling sick. Maybe it's Mother Nature's way of taking care of this baby.

**It can be comforting to know
your head doesn't have to make
all the decisions in this pregnancy.
Let your stomach talk, too.**

---

*The Lord is my shepherd, I shall not want . . .
You prepare a table before me
in the presence of my enemies . . . Psalm 23:1,5*

Mommy or Mama or What?

My mother never wanted us to call her "Mom," because that's how a boy in her grade school referred to his mother who was fat! I wonder what incidents will jump out of my hidden memories when my baby starts talking to or about me?

Will she call me Mom or Mother? Will he call me Mama or Mommy? Or will she make up her own name, unique to our family? I guess he won't call me Sandy—or will he?

Actually, I can't imagine being called anything by this child! Belonging to a baby—and hearing that expressed by my baby's name for me—is more than I can believe. I am to be deeply honored.

**What seeps into your soul
when you hear the word "Mommy"?**

Honor your father and your mother . . .
Deuteronomy 5:16

Never Again

I am sure that I never want to be pregnant again. Feeling sick all day, week after week, with the prospect of the same kind of days for yet another month or two, feels like a ridiculous thing to do to oneself on purpose! I'm sure that continuous nausea is not the best companion to rational thinking, but I doubt that I'll ever forget this awful feeling. As long as I remember it, a second pregnancy falls into the category of the absurd.

Along with pregnancy, however, must come the grace to forget, because lots of women do have more than one child—on purpose!

I'm ready to add variety to this experience. When all I know of pregnancy is nausea, I have no interest in getting myself into it again.

**Life has always offered variety.
This, too, will end.**

*Do not remember the former things,
or consider the things of old.*
Isaiah 43:18

After I wore myself out with complaining yesterday and deciding never to travel this path again, I started thinking about other times when I've felt hopeless. Whenever I'm sick or depressed, I am sure the feeling will never end. I'll be stuck in this rut forever. I'll never have a carefree feeling again. I can't even remember what happiness is like.

As I look back on those times, however, I see that I did live past them. In retrospect, they don't seem as overwhelming. In fact, when I survey my entire life, the happy times outnumber the sad times by far. It gives me a new perspective on this trimester. It's definitely miserable, but it's only one out of three. It has to get better, doesn't it?

**Remember times in your past
when you came out of
hard or painful times.**

---

*. . . everlasting joy shall be upon their heads;
they shall obtain joy and gladness,
and sorrow and sighing shall flee away.*
Isaiah 51:11

Companionship

I can't believe it! One of my friends told me that when she was pregnant, she had a craving for cheese puffs. She used to buy a bag and eat them all in one day.

I can't believe it because I did the same thing last week, but I wasn't going to admit it! The only difference was that I made myself save the second half of the bag for the next afternoon because my head said, "This is a stupid thing to feed your baby," and my husband said, "How can you eat those puffed up preservatives?"

This isn't something that can be easily explained. John didn't really want an answer anyway, so I didn't give him one. I also didn't tell him about the next bag I bought.

Find companions with whom you can enjoy the oddities of pregnancy.

. . . Who will contend with me?
Let us stand up together . . .
Isaiah 50:8

Selfishness

With the announcement of my pregnancy came the same announcement from another woman. I hardly know her, but a lot of my friends do. So now I can't talk to them about my experiences without hearing comparisons. I find myself sharing all my new-found glory with a stranger, which isn't fair because this is her third pregnancy.

At first I thought it was an insignificant coincidence that this woman's due date is the same as mine. Now I'm getting irritated because she's stealing my chance to be unique! My friends think I should get together with her so we can "compare notes." I don't want to compare notes with her. I want to be special by myself.

**Contemplate the all-encompassing love
of the One who created and sustains you.**

---

*Your eyes beheld my unformed substance.
In your book were written all the days
that were formed for me,
when none of them as yet existed.*
Psalm 139:16

Week of Last Miscarriage

I'm nervous. This is the week I miscarried in my last pregnancy. I try to block the memory from my mind, hoping that will keep it from happening again. But it's still inside there and keeps knocking for attention. What if . . . ? What if . . . .? What if . . . ?

The miscarriage was awful. The pain was worse than any cramps I've ever experienced. Going to the hospital to be sure everything was gone was not the life-giving trip I had hoped to make there. The emotional loss is still with me. My baby would be 20 months old now. I just want this week to be over.

**Let your mind,
as well as your body,
be transformed with hope.**

---

*[Jesus] will transform the body of our humiliation
that it may be conformed
to the body of his glory . . .*
Philippians 3:21

Irritation

$\mathcal{J}$t's another tearful sort of day, but I haven't let the tears out much. Some say that stopped-up tears cause colds, which is just what I don't need again, since I want to save all my sick days for my maternity leave.

Nothing seems really worth taking the time to cry over. I found a bunch of bills that had gotten stashed under the junk mail, and now I'm going to be billed for late payments. I got a notice to appear for jury duty, which I dread. I lost my library books that are due today, and I was late for everything I was supposed to do.

All this might seem insignificant, and even funny, in the long run, but my fuse feels pretty short today. The fact that my hormones are messing with my emotional stability is just one more irritation. Photographers of those little cherub baby faces should be made to list the side effects of pregnancy right under those toothless grins.

**Think of the stable factors in your life
for which you can be thankful.**

---

*Those who trust in the Lord are like Mount Zion,
which cannot be moved, but abides forever.*
Psalm 125:1

New Room

Today I told the people at work that I'm going to be a mom, and I'm still reeling from their reactions. They were more excited than I am! My joy is often tempered by my ongoing fear of a possible miscarriage, exhaustion, and nausea. Their joy, however, was not toned down by anything! It was pure and strong.

Each in his or her own way told me how wonderful parenthood is and how much I'm going to love it. I felt like I was suddenly ushered into a new room of their lives—a room they had never shown me before. Maybe they didn't want to brag about a grandeur I hadn't yet experienced. Maybe they knew I wouldn't have understood the beauty until I began building one of those rooms in my own house.

**Let the house of your life be filled
with holiness.**

---

*. . . holiness befits your house,
O Lord, forevermore.*
Psalm 93:5

Scared

I've thought a lot about this new step into parenthood since experiencing my co-workers' excitement about my news. At first I thought adding a child was like adding a new room to my house. I still don't know what it will look like, exactly, but I'm starting to realize that it won't be just a tacked-on room. This event is going to change my whole house.

This child is going to drag her toys out into the living room, play with my cooking pans, jump on my bed, park her little shoes by the door, play number games on my computer, and cover the sides of the tub with rubber duckie toys! Even before this child can move an inch, our whole home and lives will be affected. This is a little scary; no, *quite* scary!

**Dedicate your whole house and life,
to the One who loves you
and your baby.**

---

*In that day the mountains shall drip sweet wine,
the hills shall flow with milk,
. . . a fountain shall come forth
from the house of the Lord . . .*
Joel 3:18

Encouragement

When I think about the pervasiveness of a child entering my life, I can do nothing but tremble with fear at the unknown and total change. Then I remember the joy expressed by my co-workers. They're all parents, and I've heard some of their ups and downs in that role. Their spontaneous responses to my announcement, though, make it clear that the good times must outweigh the rough times. Otherwise they wouldn't have been so excited at the prospect of me entering this experience. No one sent me a sympathy card.

My fears of the future attack hardest on the days I'm the most sick or tired. I need the encouragement of the "old pros" now—and probably forever.

**Let the encouragement of others
seep all the way through you,
so your baby can feel it, too.**

*. . . I am like a green olive tree
in the house of God . . .*
Psalm 52:8

Dry

I feel totally uncreative! I have lots of wonderful things to do this weekend: a dinner party with good friends tonight, time to write or sew or read my new book, fresh bulbs to design and plant in a flower garden, and a new bread recipe to try. But I don't feel like doing any of it. Exciting options hang empty all around me because I have no motivation. Balloons of opportunity lose their air and fall around the chair where I'm glued.

I read recently that one of my favorite writers, Madeleine L'Engle, never sold anything she wrote while she was pregnant. Now I understand that. There's a little comfort for my own dryness. But I still don't like it.

**Contentment does not have to be defined
by how much fun or creativity
goes along with it.**

---

*Open to me the gates of righteousness,
that I may enter through them
and give thanks to the Lord.*
Psalm 118:19

The Bog

I feel like a big bog that can't move. I jiggle a little when the alarm goes off, just enough to figure out what day it is. If I don't have to get up right away, I sink back down and become part of the mattress again.

I'm in a dream where I'm trying to get away, but I can't move. I try to scream and nothing comes out. I rub my eyes, yet everything stays blurred. I can't listen to my mind when it tells me to get moving and be productive.

I need to get a new job with fewer hours. But who's going to hire me with my belly sticking out?

**Let go of thinking much,
doing much,
and relying on your self-sufficiency.**

---

*I will appoint Peace
as your overseer.*
Isaiah 60:17

Protective

One of my friends told me in passing today that if I have a daughter, she's going to borrow her every once in a while. Well, it may have been "in passing" for her, but it gripped my attention and blocked the rest of what she said completely. How dare she just announce that she's going to borrow my baby like she would borrow a cup of sugar? No one is borrowing this baby!

She has a six-year-old boy and is a single mom at 38 years of age. So her chances of having the girl she's longed for aren't good, but does she forget how protective she was as a new mom? Maybe she wasn't. Maybe I'm over-reacting. I wonder how I will find a good balance and attitude in letting others share the joy of my baby.

**Mom's the boss—
even if she's over-protective
by the standards of some.**

*. . . Will you question me about my children,
or command me concerning
the work of my hands?*
Isaiah 45:11

Sharing

My friend's statement about wanting to borrow my baby set me on the defensive. My immediate reaction was to keep the baby as far away from her as possible. This is my baby to take care of by myself!

How far can I take that, though? I know some people who won't let anyone else pick up their babies, and I don't want to be that sensitive. I'm charged, as a parent, with being my baby's protector, but I don't want to be too protective—or selfish.

May I not lose sight of the fact that my baby is a gift, not only to me, but to the world. Realistically, I know I can't be a mother in isolation. My baby and I will both be healthier as we participate in the lives of others and let them share in ours.

That still doesn't tell me where to draw the line regarding how much to let others in. I guess there are no easy answers I can learn from a book.

**Pray for daily guidance
rather than immediate answers.**

---

*Thus says the Lord, your Redeemer,
who formed you in the womb:
I am the Lord, who made all things . . .*
Isaiah 44:24

Wonder

I've been acting, for the last couple of days, like I'm going to have total control over my baby's socialization. It will be up to me to decide how much of this baby's time gets spent with whom.

Now I'm learning that my time of control will likely be short-lived. My baby will have a unique personality and will quickly help to decide the who, what, and when of where to spend its time, without my deliberating about it all.

I realized that when I heard a friend talking about how different her two- and four-year-olds are. Her four-year-old has always, from birth, wanted to be interacting with others. She begs every day to invite friends over. Her two-year-old, on the other hand, has always been content to be alone.

**When you find yourself
carefully calculating the future,
take a break
and let Someone else be in charge.**

---

*And now the Lord says,
who formed me in the womb to be his servant . . .
I will give you as a light to the nations . . .*
Isaiah 49:5,6

Life Insurance

Maybe I'm still too young to be sensible, or too naive to think through issues of reality, but I've never given much thought to having life insurance. I've always dismissed inquiries from salesmen by reasoning that most people in the world don't have life insurance, and many of them are poorer than I am. Besides, I can work to support myself if my husband dies.

Becoming a parent, however, is putting new thoughts of responsibility into my head. I'm bringing a new life into this world, who will be dependent on me. Maybe I need to make provisions for how this baby will survive if I die. What a horrible and unfamiliar thought! It suddenly seems important, though, to at least think about it.

**What are the blessings
you can already prepare
for your child's life?**

*Then Isaac called Jacob and blessed him . . .
May God Almighty bless you
and make you fruitful and numerous,
that you may become a company of peoples.*
Genesis 28:1,3

Guardians

aybe even more important than thinking about having life insurance is to think about the people I would want to take care of our baby if John and I would die. Money, while essential, can't replace the values and personalities that will touch this baby.

Of course, as I consider my friends and relatives, no person, family, or situation is perfect. I give up quickly, deciding the best option is to just stay alive! Okay, I'm not naive enough to really think I have control over that, but the difficulty of choosing whom I would want to raise my child, if I can't, is real.

Maybe I would do well to select someone who has a strong prayer life. If they accept the responsibility of taking over my family upon my death, I can be sure they'll pray often for a long life for me!

**Think about the values
that are important to you to pass on—
through either yourself or someone else.**

---

*You must follow exactly the path
that the Lord your God has commanded you,
so that you may live, and that it may go well with you . . .*
Deuteronomy 5:33

Guidance

For someone who is supposed to be on the way to being the strong, stabilizing force in another person's life, I feel like a failure. I'm far from having figured out all my own answers in life, and now someone else will be looking to me for answers. I'm going to be a mom, and all I want is for someone to mother me!

One good part of being so painfully conscious of one's own weakness is the freedom to admit it. That doesn't always seem like a strength, but when I feel weak, I see my need for God's guidance most clearly. When I know I can't do it alone, I am more open to the strength of my Creator carrying me, which now includes my baby.

Accept your lack of perfection.

You are indeed my rock and my fortress;
for your name's sake lead me and guide me.
Psalm 31:3

Big Things in Little Packages

I remember when one of my childhood mentors tried to convince me that some of the best things in life come in small packages. I remember, because I knew I was being selfish while appearing to be kind when my little sister and I were offered two gifts, and I chose the smaller one. It didn't work though. Hers turned out to be the better one.

So I've never really believed that theory about big things coming in little packages . . . until now. My baby is now about 1¼ inches long, weighs about ⅓ of an ounce, is nearly imperceptible to my eye, and yet is the biggest, most wonderful gift I've ever had in my life!

**See the beauty
in small things today.**

---

*Sing for joy,
O heavens, and exult,
O earth; break forth,
O mountains, into singing!
For the Lord has comforted his people . . .*
Isaiah 49:13

Bonding Fears

What if I don't like my child? I've seen some pretty bratty kids, which is probably one reason I've put off having my own as long as I have!

Or what if my baby's ugly? Some people think all babies are cute, but that hasn't always been my opinion. I hope I think mine is cute, even if other people don't.

Mothers talk about immediately bonding with their babies at birth, but what if I'm the exception? It always takes me a while to get to know someone. This is not like shopping, where I can choose what I'm going to live with for a long time!

God, help me to like my child.

Do not fear,
for you will not be ashamed . . .
Isaiah 54:4

For the first time in my life I can have sex without worrying about or trying to get pregnant! I've longed for a time like this, and now that I have it I couldn't care less. It would be okay with me to just forget that our bodies are capable of joining.

I feel selfish, though. It's too bad men don't experience the same pregnancy symptoms sexually as their wives. It's also too bad that some women react to pregnancy by feeling more passionate than ever. It's too bad because it looks like I'm not one of those dream women—at least not this trimester.

**"Normal"
is whatever is right for you.**

---

*My beloved is mine and I am his; . . .
until the day breathes and the shadows flee,
turn, my beloved,
be like a gazelle or a young stag on the cleft mountains.*
Song of Solomon 2:16,17

Walking Comatose

I love to listen to my husband talking on the phone. I especially like it when he's saying nice things about his wife! I often learn more about him when I pretend not to be listening. He says things in different ways than he tells me, or he talks about feelings and thoughts he assumes I already know.

Last night was one such moment of enlightenment. I heard him tell his sister that I have turned into a "walking comatose." I reacted by planning to tell him all the things his "comatose" wife had gotten done that day. By the time he got off the phone, though, I had rolled over on the couch and fallen back to sleep.

**Sleep as much as possible,
unapologetically.
Your body is working overtime.**

---

*For the Lord has poured out upon you
a spirit of deep sleep . . .*
Isaiah 29:10

Part of the Team

*C*ould it be the delineation of the sexes that keeps me, and any other human, from being God? I cannot create another human life by myself. With the invention of artificial means of conception, a woman no longer needs the presence of a man in her life to become impregnated, but she cannot do it alone, either. Only God created alone.

I feel humbled today, in a grand sort of way, to be just one part of the creation that is within me. I am hosting the beginnings of this person, but, even now, I am not solely responsible. I am gifted with the bodily functions of conceiving and bearing. I am gifted with a partner who entrusted me with his holy seed. I am gifted with the growing seed. I am gifted with the mental and emotional capacity to be part of this team.

**When you feel alone,
think of the others in your team of creating.**

---

*. . . you have made [human beings]
a little lower than God,
and crowned them with glory and honor.*
Psalm 8:5

Miscarriage

I got a call from my best friend tonight. She had gone to the doctor for her usual checkup at 17 weeks, and they couldn't find a heartbeat. The doctor said the baby may have been dead for a week. The next morning she started having labor pains, and the baby was soon expelled. She said he fit in her palm—a complete baby who was clearly a boy.

I haven't been able to stop shaking. I don't know whether I'm more sad for her or scared for me. She was farther along in her pregnancy than I am. A miscarriage is not supposed to happen at 17 weeks. It's not ever supposed to happen.

Lord, have mercy.
Christ, have mercy.

Have mercy on me, O God,
according to your steadfast love . . .
Psalm 51:1

More on Miscarriage

When I tell people that my friend had a miscarriage, they say what I guess they think are comforting words like, "Maybe he would have been deformed or mentally incapacitated." "Maybe it was God's way of saving your friend and her baby from pain that we don't know about."

Or they ask questions like, "Well, she already has two children, doesn't she?" and "Will she try to get pregnant again?"

I don't know the answers to these questions, but I hope they don't say any of them to my friend. She held her dead son in her hand, and that's all that matters right now. She's not living in the healing future. She's living the painful present.

**Pray for a mother who has lost her baby,
even if it seems to you
like it was a long time ago.**

*A voice was heard in Ramah,
wailing and loud lamentation,
Rachel weeping for her children;
she refused to be consoled, because they are no more.*
Matthew 2:18

Twins

They want to test me to determine whether or not I'm having twins. I never thought of that possibility. John and I decided to have a baby; maybe more would fit in the picture later. We never talked about having more than one at a time, though!

When I was little I always thought it would be fun to be and have a twin. But, suddenly, in this role in the family, the idea is not so appealing. Double diapers? Double stroller? Two cribs? With both hands full, I'd have none left to do anything else. Who would feed me?

No, twins are not my first choice. But then, no one's offering me a choice!

**Grant me patience, Lord,
to endure my blessings.**

---

*When you send forth your spirit,
they are created,
and you renew the face of the ground.*
Psalm 104:30

Morning Hole

$\mathcal{G}$ have no desire for my usual (well, it was usual until four months ago) cup of coffee to start the day, but this new morning ritual—feeling nauseated—is an extremely poor substitute! I long for some comforting way to soothe my soul and warm me, as coffee often did. I miss the coziness of coffee smells coming from the kitchen and the gurgling way our ancient coffeepot greeted the morning. At the same time, I'm thankful that John has agreed to get his coffee at work until my aversion to it is past.

The hole remains, though. Morning is now something to endure and to get over as fast as possible, rather than a tranquil time to relish.

**Be creative in filling the
hole left by pregnancy symptoms:
soothing music,
more time in bed,
a bubble bath,
a new kind of cracker . . .**

---

*You will forget your misery;
you will remember it as waters
that have passed away.*
Job 11:16

Mother Forever

When we were first deciding about whether or not to have children, I thought in terms of a 20-year commitment. Today in the mail, I got a present from my parents. It reminded me that, no matter how far apart we live, my parents have always celebrated my birthday, Children's Day, Valentine's Day, Christmas, and a few holidays that they make up, just because they want to give me something.

The reality of motherhood being a lifetime commitment is just beginning to sink in. Sometimes it's a scary thought; sometimes it's wonderful!

**Imagine yourself rooted in the long,
overlapping heritage of motherhood.**

*The man named his wife Eve,
because she was the mother of all living.*
Genesis 3:20

Headaches

My head is pounding so hard I can't think straight. I don't usually like to take medication when I'm sick, but now that pregnancy prevents me from taking the usual over-the-counter "cures," I want them! I guess this is one more symptom that lets me know there are hormonal, physical, and emotional changes going on in my life in preparation for this baby. I'd prefer a less painful sign.

Maybe it's also a sign of today's stress. I was unusually busy, running from one thing to the next all day. If I had watched this happen to a friend, I'd tell her to go rest her eyes in a dark and quiet room. Maybe I'll be my own friend.

Compensate for the unavailable remedy of pills by being gentle with yourself.

. . . I will say,
"Peace be within you."
Psalm 122:8

Contradictions

I feel like I'm a living, breathing, growing contradiction. I'm sick (literally) of being pregnant. I love being pregnant.

I can't wait to be a mother. I'm scared spitless of being a mother. I get so excited I can't stop talking. I cry the next moment and can't imagine that I'll ever be happy again. Yesterday I lovingly hung my husband's shirt up in the closet. Today I yelled at him for being sloppy. (I'm sure the color of the shirt thrown across the bed didn't make that much difference.)

I can't believe pregnancy has changed me this much! If I don't use pregnancy as an excuse, my emotional health is in big trouble! Sometimes I'm glad for something to blame. Today, however, I refuse to give it that much power. I just want to be myself again.

**Ask your best friend
if you look as contradictory as you feel.**

---

*On God rests my deliverance and my honor;
my mighty rock, my refuge is in God.*
Psalm 62:7

Isolation

While I like the idea of asking my best friend how I've been acting lately, I have a hard time thinking whom to ask. With the ups and downs of my emotions during the last couple months, I've kept to myself a lot.

I'm not comfortable making plans to get together with someone when I can't predict if I'll be grumpy or fun to be with by the time evening comes. I don't invite anyone for supper when I can't think of anything to cook. I don't accept invitations because I'm afraid I won't be able to eat what they serve. I haven't given my friends a chance to know me much lately. I guess I have isolated myself!

**Isolation can be a healthy or a bad habit.
Evaluate your social needs
and make appropriate plans.**

*. . . O God, be merciful to me,
for in you my soul takes refuge;
in the shadow of your wings I will take refuge,
until the destroying storms pass by.*
Psalm 57:1

Intuition

$\mathcal{I}$ just realized that this is the weekend of the conference I was asked to participate in a year ago. For some reason, I didn't feel like it was the right thing for me to do when I received the invitation. I had no logical reason to say no. It would have been interesting to attend, and it was an honor to be asked to be one of the speakers. It didn't seem right, though, so I declined.

I've felt more sick and miserable these last two weeks than I have for a long time—the time when I would have needed to do the most intense preparation for that conference. I'm not sure how I could be concentrating right now on anything more demanding than what food will most likely stay down.

I'm so glad I listened to my intuition last year. I don't want to think about anything!

**Give thanks for how God
speaks through your intuition.
Let it guide you again today.**

---

*Who among you fears the Lord
and obeys the voice of his servant,
who walks in darkness and has no light,
yet trusts in the name of the Lord
and relies upon his God?*
Isaiah 50:10

Normal?

Will I ever be normal again? That question keeps sliding into my brain. Sometimes it refers to my body shape and weight. Sometimes it's in reference to my energy level. Sometimes I'm thinking about my new range of emotions and their unpredictability.

The answers that keep coming back to that question are "No, no, and no." I won't ever be normal again because my body is going through some wild gyrations. My energy level will forevermore be split with another primary relationship, who will also affect my emotions. If I feel a great need to be normal, it looks like I'll have to change the definition.

Enjoy the fun part of being forever changed— the part that makes you feel uniquely needed.

For everything there is a season . . .
a time to seek, and a time to lose . . .
Ecclesiastes 3:1,6

Gift of Sleep

Sleep has always seemed like a waste of time to me. I feel like the four-year-old who asked her mother if children have anything, like adults have coffee, to keep them awake. She wanted to hear one more story, but could hardly keep her eyes open. Life is too short and full of excitement to spend it sleeping.

I was always jealous of my grandpa who never needed more than six hours of sleep. I'm miserable without eight. Now, of course, even eight doesn't satisfy my insatiable appetite for sleep.

If I can trust the baby books, however, this, too, will pass. Maybe I should just receive the need as a gift, and, while I have a good excuse, live it up (or down!).

**Accept the rest your body deserves
and consider yourself, thereby,
God's beloved.**

---

*It is vain that you rise up early and go late to rest,
eating the bread of anxious toil;
for he gives sleep to his beloved.*
Psalm 127:2

Angels

Mother is starting to send me things she's had stored away in her attic since I was a baby. She saved them for 30 years, secretly moving them with her from house to house, waiting for the moment I would cherish them rather than throw them away in my attempts to grow up or declare myself independent.

She saved my baby blankets and first clothes, cards received at my birth, and pictures that hung on my walls. I unwrapped a painting today that I vividly remember. It's an angel watching over two children playing, oblivious to their protector. I remember finding comfort in that picture as a child. I find comfort in it again today, because I already know I'm not going to be able to take care of this baby all by myself.

**Give thanks for the angels
who are helping to guard
your growing family.**

---

*Bless the Lord,
O you his angels,
you mighty ones who do his bidding . . .*
Psalm 103:20

Give and Receive

Another treasure my mother recently passed on to me from my childhood is a journal she kept about me during the first four years of my life. Some of the things she wrote, especially after I could talk, are hilarious. My interactions with my siblings are fun. The insights into how I learned to perceive the world are fascinating. Reading about the joy I added to the family is heartwarming.

I have been thinking a lot about how much time and energy this baby is going to take from me. The sudden changes in John's and my lifestyle and the demands of one so tiny and dependent will be strenuous, no doubt.

I hadn't thought much, however, about the new entertainment center that's moving in. I will have a new person to watch who will be both fascinating and fun. I will laugh at my growing child, and my heart will surely be warmed many times.

**Thank God for the joy
of what you will receive through your child.**

---

*But the steadfast love of the Lord
is from everlasting to everlasting on those who fear him,
and his righteousness to children's children.*
Psalm 103:17

Replication

I find myself absentmindedly worrying about my child growing up to be disobedient or mean or socially deviant. It feels like a huge risk to bring a child into the world. I might have some control over what my baby and toddler do, but I know my control will be increasingly limited after that. Why am I opening myself to such horrendous possibilities?

I could, instead, dream about the influence I will likely always have in the life of my child. I've gotten a lot of good values and traits from my parents, which they emulated and drew from their parents and grandparents. So why wouldn't my child want to continue the cycle of living a godly life? I am opening myself to such exciting and precious possibilities!

Which of your values and/or character traits do you hope your child replicates?

I am reminded of your sincere faith,
a faith that lived first
in your grandmother Lois and your mother Eunice
and now, I am sure, lives in you.
II Timothy 1:5

Women Complete

I've heard mothers say that they never felt complete until they had their first baby. I never understood that. I felt complete before I was pregnant, most of the time. When I didn't, it wasn't because I hadn't had a baby. It was because I hadn't finished a degree or taken a trip I longed to go on, or that a relationship was breaking.

I've been worried that having a baby would make me feel more fragmented, rather than being relieved that I will finally be complete.

But now that having a baby has become a reality within my very body, I do feel more whole than I ever longed to be! I'm living out one more potential of my womanhood. And what a huge one it is!

**Take a moment
to reflect on the wonder of living
in this big potential of your womanhood.**

---

*. . . [Rachel] said to Jacob,
"Give me children, or I shall die!"*
Genesis 30:1

Men Complete

*I*f having a baby is part of feeling complete for a woman, how can a man feel like a complete person without having a baby? I don't know any men who don't feel complete because they can't bear children. In fact, I heard a man say last week that if it were up to him to carry the children, he and his wife would not have any!

Many women long for the experience, while men seem to be satisfied with merely influencing the genes. Maybe God created me, not only with the potential, but also with the proper accompanying desire. I guess that's not so hard to believe!

**Thank you, God,
for the longing you've put within me
to carry this child.**

For this child I prayed . . .
I Samuel 1:27

Pervasive Pregnancy

This must be the year to be pregnant! Everywhere I look I see a pregnant woman—in the grocery store, at the museum, in front of me at church, at work. The only time I noticed this many pregnant women before was when I wanted to be pregnant and wasn't!

It feels like a little community, dispersed into the rest of the world, acting like we're normal to everyone else, but we know better. We smile at each other and know that we're special. We are not just one more statistic embodying another. We are each unique, carrying a secret about which others can see only the outer effects.

**Pray for the last pregnant woman
you encountered.**

. . . My soul magnifies the Lord.
Luke 1:46

DINKS

On the Sunday newspaper this week was a disconcerting article about DINKS—Double Income No Kids. One of the couples, when asked what they did with all their time and money not being used by kids, said they go on two vacations each year and eat out four times a week!

Even though our incomes haven't allowed us quite that degree of pleasure, we have nearly guaranteed that that kind of freedom and luxury is unlikely to ever happen to us! Our flirtation with being DINKS is quickly coming to an end. And we are about to give up some pretty nice things in our relatively free lives!

**Plan to savor a leisurely meal
at your favorite restaurant sometime soon!**

---

*Do not be afraid, little flock,
for it is your Father's good pleasure
to give you the kingdom.*
Luke 12:32

Fear

I didn't want to admit to John that I am sometimes afraid of having a baby. I didn't want him
to think I've changed my mind and don't want a
baby anymore.

When I finally got up the nerve to say it out loud,
though, it didn't seem so awful. He understands why
I'm afraid that we won't have enough time alone
anymore and that we will drift apart. I'm afraid of
what a baby will do to our sex life, our sleep life, my
solitude. Those weren't pleasant feelings to admit,
but I was relieved to know that the reason he
understands is because he has the same fears himself!

**Are you keeping your fears
bottled up inside?**

---

*For I, the Lord your God, hold your right hand:
it is I who say to you,
"Do not fear, I will help you."*
Isaiah 41:13

Sharing Fear

One of the reasons I was afraid to talk about my fears was because I thought if I voiced them, they would get worse. They felt like a fungus, ready to stealthily grow in every crevice of my life if I let them out of their dark, tightly wrapped package.

Amazingly, though, when I shared them with John, I felt bright companionship, and the light started melting them down to a size with which I can more easily live. I prefer having them in front of me where they look normal, instead of letting them lurk inside where they threaten to disturb the peace of my marriage and my baby.

**Find a friend with whom to share
one of your fears.**

Do not fear, for I am with you . . .
Isaiah 41:10

Fear Exposed

$\mathcal{I}$ learned, as I talked to John about my fears, that when I don't bring them up, they still affect our relationship. I was afraid our baby would come between us, but my unwillingness to talk about that was already coming between us. I was both fearing and creating the distance!

This is all strange for me. I've experienced fear before, and usually I verbalize my feelings easily. This event seems bigger, though, somehow. It's a life I'm talking about. It's the biggest responsibility I've ever had. The fear is too deep for words, and I've been going inside to meet it, rather than calling it out to meet me, where I have the support of others.

**Thank you, God,
that I'm not really in this alone,
even when I feel like I am.**

---

*And Mary remained with [Elizabeth]
about three months . . .*
Luke 1:56

"Do Not Be Afraid"

When I read about Mary, the mother of Jesus, her fear seems to be dispelled in one easy command from the angel—"Fear not." She consents, at the end of their short conversation, to be the servant of the Lord, whatever that entailed.

The Bible doesn't record, however, how many times Mary went back to those words for comfort. I wonder how many times she had to lean on, "Fear not," during her young teenage pregnancy, the journey to Bethlehem, having no room in an inn to deliver the child, on their flight into Egypt, throughout her marriage, single parenting after Joseph's death, and the life and death of her own son? I wonder how often she had to remind herself of that first encounter with the angel? Often, I'll bet.

Receive the angel's words of comfort to Mary, for yourself.

The angel said to her,
"Do not be afraid, Mary . . . "
Luke 1:30

Favored of God

The angel also told Mary that she had found favor with God. What had Mary done in her short life to receive such an honor? What were her parents and her childhood like? How did she get to be so selfless?

Samuel of the Old Testament also seemed to hear and accept God's command with little effort. These younger people seemed to be able to easily accept the will of God when they were called—something grown men, like Moses and Jonah failed to do.

Maybe I try too hard, sometimes, to be grown-up. Maybe I dwell too much on all my faults; those are the times when I doubt that I can be a good mother. Maybe God finds favor with me more easily than I find favor with myself.

**You, too,
are favored by God.**

---

*The angel said to [Mary],
" . . . you have found favor with God."*
Luke 1:30

Jealousy

I can still see the picture in my mind of my husband cuddling a cat, soon after we recognized our attraction to each other. A streak of jealousy lashed out from me at that cat and all other potential cats in his life! I decided then that I never wanted a cat in my home. I find it easier to say that I don't like cats, than to admit that I'm afraid a cat will take some of the cuddling that would otherwise be lavished on me!

Even though our love has matured beyond those first days of infatuation, I wonder what having another person to hold will do to us. John could already be jealous that so much of my energy is turned inward, nurturing the forming of our baby. I could be jealous of the father-child duo, even though I long to watch it happen. I hope I won't be.

**Talk about your feelings as they surface—
pretty or not.**

*. . . Love is not envious or boastful or arrogant or rude.
It does not insist on its own way;
it is not irritable or resentful.*
I Corinthians 13:4,5

Prolonged PMS

I feel like I've had pre-menstrual syndrome for three months now. It was bad enough when two or three days of the month whirled me into a turbulence of emotional lows, when I wondered how life could get so bad so fast. The only good part was that I realized what was happening, knew when it was coming, and anticipated when it would end. This time, though, it isn't going away!

I wonder if this is where the tradition of pregnant women staying at home got its start. No one else wanted to be around their mood swings, and the women themselves were embarrassed by their unpredictable natures as well! I wish I could stay home and sleep all day.

**Give yourself a break from being sociable.
Don't even pressure yourself
to provide an excuse.**

*For a long time I have held my peace,
I have kept still and restrained myself;
now I will cry out like a woman in labor . . .*
Isaiah 42:14

Hair and Nails

From now on, when I find out that a friend is pregnant, I'm going to congratulate her with a nail clippers and shaver. No one ever told me that pregnancy makes nails and hair grow faster!

It makes sense, with the increase in blood flow, but it's just one more thing that caught me off-guard. I used to think I knew my body. Suddenly, I feel caught somewhere between awe and horror at being taken over like this.

But then, it's really not so different from all of life. Even doctors will never know everything about how human bodies work. Pregnancy is just a variation on a theme, with which I was only partially familiar—life in this body.

**Give special thanks
for one part of your "new" body.**

---

*For it was you
who formed my inward parts . . .*
Psalm 139:13

Pushy Doctor

At first I really liked my doctor. She is a bold, strong-willed German woman, who left no doubt in my mind that she knew what she was doing. Furthermore, she knew what I was going to do, too. I liked that, especialy on my first visit, because I had all questions and no answers. I was glad someone was in control.

By my second and third visits, I had done more reading and was less comforted by her short and sure answers. I wanted someone knowledgeable who would also listen to my intuitions.

This month, when she said I had to take a blood test that I later found out was optional, I decided it was time to change doctors. She may know a lot more than I do about many things, but she's not God. I need to take some control back into my own hands.

**Believe in yourself enough
to not be pushed around,
even by professionals.**

---

*But my eyes are turned toward you,
O God, my Lord;
in you I seek refuge;
do not leave me defenseless.*
Psalm 141:8

Contentment

For a woman who has often found pride in accomplishing many things, I'm surprised that I am currently content to simply be. I can sit quietly for an entire evening, reading from my stack of books about pregnancy, without needing to write a letter or call a friend.

When I think about my pre-pregnancy days, colors flash around me in a blur. I wanted to stay busy, to be with friends, to keep my calendar full. Now I feel like the center of my world has moved inside me. The busy life of fun and excitement has turned into a beautiful, settling contentment.

**Meditate on what is
at the center of your life.**

*. . . there is great gain in godliness
combined with contentment.*
I Timothy 6:6

Expectant Father

Sometimes I get lost in a cozy world of my baby and me moving together to our own rhythms, and I forget that I'm living with an expectant father, too. I heard one of his friends ask him today if he's gaining weight with me, like a lot of men do.

We all laughed because John hasn't varied his weight more than one or two pounds since the day I met him. I wonder, though, if he's experiencing other pregnancy symptoms as his way of being part of this whole process. Some studies have found that half of all expectant fathers experience some kind of sympathetic symptoms.

Come to think of it, he was feeling nauseated a few weeks ago. Morning sickness, maybe?

Ask your baby's father
how he's doing with the adjustment
to impending fatherhood.

Let each of you look not to your own interests,
but to the interests of others.
Philippians 2:4

Sympathetic Symptoms

I can understand how expectant fathers would have sympathetic pregnancy symptoms when I think about how my own imagination and stress influence my body. During every month when I thought I might be pregnant but didn't yet know, I was nauseous with hope.

My belly already looked bigger. I was obsessed with eating the right foods and my back ached. I felt more tired than usual, and I was sure I was pregnant. When I see a friend being sick, I often feel sick myself. So I guess a father under stress from pregnancy isn't so strange.

**Offer to give your husband
a back rub.**

---

*If one member suffers,
all suffer together with it . . .*
I Corinthians 12:26

Cravings

I never thought I'd succumb to the outrageous cravings of pregnancy. Pickles with ice cream? Not me! I'm a little more in control and level-headed than that.

But I should know by now that my body is not sitting around waiting for instructions from my calculating little brain. Rather, my brain is racing to keep me up-to-date with what's happening to my body and the baby's!

It just happened again. Without understanding it as a craving, I have been eating a lot more meat than usual. Today I read that at this point in my pregnancy, my body needs more protein. Now how could my body know that and take care of itself without letting my brain in on the strategies? It's simply amazing!

**Let your brain take directions
from your intuition—
at least temporarily.**

*My frame was not hidden from you,
when I was being made in secret,
intricately woven
in the depths of the earth.*
Psalm 139:15

Peacefulness

Before I became pregnant, I read that a mother's disposition can affect her baby from the moment of conception. That gave me considerable reason to worry, because I'm the kind of person who thrives under stress. I don't always like it, but so far in my life I've done more to build stress than to relieve it. I must be getting something out of it! I was scared to see what that might produce in an infant.

Now the season in question has arrived, and I've never felt so peaceful in my life! I feel like I'm already living inside of me with my baby. Events and other people's attitudes or actions don't have the power to upset me anymore. I'm just not letting any of it in!

**Let the peacefulness
with which your baby floats inside of you,
seep into your center as well.**

---

*The Lord bless you and keep you; . . .
the Lord lift up his countenance upon you,
and give you peace.*
Numbers 6:24,26

To Know or Not to Know the Sex

fter "When are you due?", the second most often asked question has to be, "Are you having a boy or a girl?" It's a relatively new question, but it's commonly asked. My parents didn't even know they could ask the question. All the people for years and years before them didn't know it could exist. So why would I want to know what sex child I'm having? Won't the element of surprise add excitement to the rest of my pregnancy?

With the means to know, though, comes heightened demands. Most of my acquaintances do find out what sex their babies are. They can plan more efficiently and only have to choose one name. The hardest part of this puzzle may be for John and me to agree on what we want to do.

**Whether or not
you decide to know the sex of your baby,
your decision will be the right one.**

---

*The vision of all this
has become for you
like the words of a sealed document . . .*
Isaiah 29:11

Needles and Tests

*I*f they stick me with one more needle or tell me I have to undergo one more test, I'll be certain that I'm an assaulted victim instead of the nurturing mother-to-be I'd like to believe I am. I'm losing the battle to be dignified as they pour awful stuff down my throat, strap my arms to a chair, stick me with needles, and proudly display my lifeblood which they extract in their little tubes. Doesn't my baby need all that blood, by the way?

My protests never make it past my heart, though, which silently gives them permission to do anything necessary to enhance my baby's life. Pregnancy is so much more complicated than I thought it would be, seeing how normal a thing it is to do, and has been, for so many generations! Oh, now I forget what they said this test was for.

**Consider yourself blessed by God
and thanked by your baby
for all the tests you are enduring.**

---

*. . . Do not be discouraged,
for you will not suffer disgrace . . .*
Isaiah 54:4

Terror

Your blood test indicates there is a slight chance your baby could be born with Downes Syndrome. We have to do more testing to determine . . . " The doctor's voice droned on behind her lowered eyes, which blurred out in front of me as panic seared through my body and took control.

They must be wrong. But what if they're not? No, you're not doing any more testing. I wish I wouldn't have let you do the first one. What good can it do now? Do you expect me to abort my baby? I've got to calm down. I can't let my baby feel all this tension!

How will I live with a baby that can never develop normally? How can this be happening to me? One chance out of 250 is low, yes, but no comfort to me, the possible mother of that $1/250$th of a chance. That's my baby we're talking about and my life. We're not statistics!

**Imagine yourself being held tightly
in the womb of God
who loves you with a fierce love.**

---

*For the Lord has called you
like a wife forsaken and grieved in spirit . . .*
Isaiah 54:6

Unspoken Dreams

I never realized how many dreams I already have for my baby, until I heard the possibility that the baby may not develop normally. No, it can't be true. I already have a dream that's painted only in my head so far, of going for walks together and teaching my child all the names of the flowers. I have a wish dream of loving my child that includes me and others and God, like I experience love. I know I can't choose a career for my child, but to have no career at all . . . ? No, God!

I want my baby to be normal. I want my baby to grow and learn. I want to watch my child become independent. I want my child to leave home some-day.

**Close your eyes
and watch the drama you've already created
for your child
in the wish dreams of your soul.**

*O afflicted one, storm-tossed, and not comforted . . .
All your children shall be taught by the Lord . . .*
Isaiah 54:11,13

Downes Syndrome

finally got up enough courage to say the words aloud. I told a good friend that the doctor said our baby might have Downes Syndrome. I expected him to become as sullen as I have been. I was jarred when his immediate response was, "That's not the worst thing that could happen!"

He didn't say it in an unkind or uncaring way. He was gentle and factual. And, suddenly, I knew he was right. Many other things could be worse.

My prayers made a definite shift from that moment on. I now pray for strength and love to face whatever this baby brings to my life, because I'm still terribly frightened.

**Accept the facts
without ignoring your heart.**

---

*For the mountains may depart
and the hills be removed,
but my steadfast love shall not depart from you . . .*
Isaiah 54:10

In Me

just got home from having my first ultrasound, from watching my baby move around in there—inside me! There really is a baby! I can't tell on the outside of me yet. Some days I've wondered if I was just having a long case of the flu.

But there it was—a live picture coming out of the camera that was pointed at me! I saw the heart beating and other parts, which I trust are arms and legs, flailing around. That baby never quit moving!

It's hard to believe I have all that life in motion inside me, yet I'm not able to feel it. I find it almost unbelievable to think it's all happening within me! That wasn't just "the baby." It's *my* baby!

**Go ahead and jump for joy
(while you still can do it easily!).**

---

*Bless the Lord, O my soul,
and all that is within me,
bless his holy name.*
Psalm 103:1

Rash Reactions

I may as well get a certificate of divorce for the duration of this pregnancy. I'm being so awful to my husband, yelling about everything he does or doesn't do. Somehow it's even his fault when I can't find anything decent to wear.

I don't mean to hurt him. Why do I hurt most the one I love the most? I need him, and I want him to need me, but he certainly doesn't need this. He has tried so hard to understand me, but I don't even understand myself.

I want my other self back. I want to regain the ability to think before I bite. I want to live out of a steady wisdom rather than these rash reactions.

**Use freely
the gift of apology.**

---

*Who has put wisdom in the inward parts,
or given understanding to the mind?*
Job 38:36

Gratefulness

This morning I read in a book about pregnancy that a lot could soon be going wrong in my body, if it hasn't begun already! During pregnancy it's normal to experience nosebleeds, nasal congestion, anemia, high blood pressure, diabetes, constipation, ear stuffiness, headaches, varicose veins, hemorrhoids, dizziness, etc., etc.

I figure I can either add all those things to my worry list and be vigilant in watching for the signs, or I can be highly grateful for the minimal effects this pregnancy is having on me—considering the possibilities. Gratefulness seems to come easiest and be the most uplifting response today.

That was an easy decision!

**For every side effect
of pregnancy that bothers you,
be grateful for two you don't have.**

---

*. . . We shall be satisfied
with the goodness of your house,
your holy temple.*
Psalm 65:4

Second Child

"The fact of this pregnancy is finally starting to sink in. I'm really pregnant, and I'm really going to have a baby! That fact is overwhelming enough by itself, but, would you believe, I'm already fantasizing about having another child?

I guess it makes sense because, even when I wasn't sure I wanted any children, I knew that if I had one, I'd want more. If I alter my life for a child, I may as well welcome another alteration. Having had siblings, I want my children to know the same knocks and fun I experienced growing up with a sister and brothers.

So with the reality of pregnancy comes the hope of another soon to follow.

**Remember the joys
of your childhood home.**

*The earth has yielded its increase;
God, our God, has blessed us.
May God continue to bless us . . .*
Psalm 67:6,7

Second Pregnancy

This can't be as hard the second time around, can it? Even if I'm nauseated for a solid three months, I'll know that the first trimester does come to an end. Maybe I'll be more accepting of the changes in my body and my lifestyle the next time, because I'll know better what to expect. Maybe I won't have to read so much since I'm learning it all now. I can spend all nine months simply enjoying the pregnancy. Maybe I won't be so scared of labor and delivery after living through it once. On the other hand, I could be more scared if this one is hard.

I could worry about that now, too, if I wanted to! No, I'll do that later . . .

One pregnancy at a time.

. . . Do not worry about tomorrow . . .
Today's trouble is enough for today.
Matthew 6:34

Pregnant Plus One

I wonder what my mother did with my brother when she was pregnant with me. He was only two years old, so she couldn't leave him alone and go take a nap every time she felt like it. He had to eat, whether or not she got sick at the thought of preparing food. He probably weighed more than she was supposed to carry, but waiting for a two-year-old to walk everywhere on his own must have been laboriously trying.

When I feel sorry for myself because of how much energy it takes to be pregnant, I'll try to remember the women who are doing it with another one already in their laps, or while helping a few others do their homework. I guess I can enjoy how selfishly I am able to spend my time and energy, at least this time.

**Life—even pregnancy—
could be so much harder!**

---

*Blessed be the Lord,
who daily bears us up . . .*
Psalm 68:19

Great With Child

I've been thinking, lately, about the physical aspects of subsequent pregnancies. Some of them would likely be harder; some easier.

I wonder, too, about the emotions of a two- or three-year-old, anticipating another child. I can imagine seeing my daughter's eyes light up with excitement when I tell her she's going to have a new baby brother or sister. She'd have fun telling her friends, and she'd jump for joy just as I'd like to but would only allow my heart to do. I'd enjoy letting her feel the baby move, assuring her that there will always be room on Mommy's lap for her.

Her joy would be mixed with jealousy, too, so she'd become even more special to me as I try to make sure she knows my love. I can already understand a little more about the pervasiveness of God's love, just imagining having more people join my own circle of love!

**Thank God for all the people
in your circle of love—present and future.**

---

*Praise the Lord, all you nations!
Extol him, all you peoples!
For great is his steadfast love toward us . . .*
Psalm 117:1,2

Concentration

I hesitate to blame my wandering mind on this pregnancy, too, like I seem to be blaming everything these days, but I wonder . . . My head isn't quite as full anymore with the constant struggle to cope with morning sickness, although occasional attacks still interrupt my days. Any rumble in the vicinity of my middle jerks my attention from whatever I'm doing, so I can figure out if it's my baby or gas. Even when no bodily functions act strangely, my brain often interrupts my work to remind me that I'm pregnant. And then nothing else seems quite as important for a few minutes.

Maybe I just need to redefine concentration. Mine has simply been more broken up, lately, into different areas. I feel like I'm not quite together, but there can't be any better reason to have my thoughts interrupted than having a baby!

When you feel like you're not quite together, remind yourself of all that is going on inside you. Know that you have never been more together in your life!

For God alone my soul waits in silence, for my hope is from him.
Psalm 62:5

Body Factory

ometimes when I think about being pregnant, I imagine my body to be a bustling factory. I envision all my organs putting in overtime to create and sustain this new little being. My blood vessels are fuller and busier than ever. My ligaments are stretching and shifting. My stomach is learning to share. My back is switching gears to carry an unfamiliar load. (My bladder is not carrying its usual weight at all!) My heart seems ready to burst from being so full of love and excitement. Instead, it just stretches, like my belly, to hold more and more.

It's hard to imagine that, on the outside, I look basically like the same person. I'm not, you know!

**Treat your body
to one of the benefits
an employee that works overtime deserves.**

. . . glorify God in your body.
I Corinthians 6:20

111

Part of the Sun

A friend sent me a wonderful birthday card today. The picture is of smiling children of all nationalities, reaching up to a brilliant splash of yellow. Inside it says, "We Love Being Part of the Sun!"

What an invitation to life!

It's a perfect image for how I feel today. I'm celebrating my entrance into the circle of life over 30 years ago, which has gone on to prepare another generation for birth. My child, too, is joining all creation in the circle of life.

God, I pray that my baby
will love being part of the sun.

For the Lord God is a sun and shield:
he bestows favor and honor . . .
Psalm 84:11

Time

In high school home economics class, we were each given an egg to take home with us one weekend. It was our "baby," and part of a simulation game to help us realize the magnitude of responsibility that comes with getting pregnant. It was intended, I suspect, to function as an "indirect" form of birth control! I spent a lot of the weekend trying to convince other people to babysit my egg so I wouldn't have to worry about it.

I don't know if my sense of motherhood has increased simply because of my age or because of the type of "egg" I now have, but I can't imagine wanting anyone to babysit this baby. I may have to use childcare, and my baby may seem like a bother sometimes, but I have a growing sense that I will want to be with my baby as much as possible.

**Is it any wonder
that God wants to be with me
all the time?**

---

*The Lord is my shepherd . . .
he makes me lie down in green pastures;
he leads me beside still waters.*
Psalm 23:1,2

Nagging Questions

I wonder, sometimes, if we should have waited to have children until we were earning more money. Are we going to be able to give this child all its necessary clothes and toys, medical care and entertainment? Will our child be emotionally scarred if we can't provide all the things other parents give their children, our child's peers?

There's a sensible voice inside me saying that quality love is more important than anything money buys. For some reason, though, the questions lurk around my confidence, as if to uproot it.

**Give your questions air time,
but don't let them steal the show.
Talk back to them.**

---

*. . . If one offered for love all the wealth of his house,
it would be utterly scorned.*
Song of Solomon 8:7

Fat or Pregnant?

This has got to be the most embarrassing stage of pregnancy. I'm not obviously pregnant yet, but it is obvious that I am bigger than before. I just look like I'm gaining weight uncontrollably.

I no longer feel like announcing my due date to everyone I meet, but I can feel people silent wondering when I pass them in the neighborhood or at the grocery store. "My she's getting fat!" they're all thinking.

Yes, it's embarrassing. On the other hand, I can't think of any better reason to be fat! I better enjoy it while I have an excuse.

**Enjoy your new look
for this season!**

---

*. . . Blessed are you among women,
and blessed is the fruit of your womb.*
Luke 1:42

Humor

It's kind of funny how each woman experiences pregnancy differently from every other woman. We have certain things in common, which is consoling when we compare the unpleasant times and fun when we talk about the good times. But each of us is unique, too, and no one can predict with certainty what the next day, or next trimester, will bring.

It's kind of funny that the doctors don't know everything, either. Sometimes I ask questions as if I expect them to, including the exact day and method of my baby's birth. If they could know more, my fears would be diminished.

It would take the mystery away, though, if everything were predictable. So, since I'm having a good day today, it's easy to keep laughing and preserve the awe.

**When you feel alone and uncertain,
look to humor
rather than knowledge for the cure.**

---

*. . . God has brought laughter for me;
everyone who hears will laugh with me.*
Genesis 21:6

CPR

Since the required CPR (cardiopulmonary resuscitation) course I took in high school, I've had no interest in remembering or relearning those safety procedures. I always figure there will be someone else nearby who is a CPR expert if the need arises. That's a rotten attitude, I know, but there it is!

I saw an advertisement in the paper this week for infant CPR. Now that produced a different reaction in me. I was suddenly scared. What if my baby choked, and I was the only one around? I wouldn't know how to do anything! What if I couldn't get help in time? What if my baby died because of my ignorance?

I'd still rather ignore the fear and hope I never need to know CPR. Looking at the alternatives, however, I grant that a few hours of training now could reduce the risk of my baby dying someday. Why take an unnecessary gamble? I'd feel worse than rotten if I needed to know it and hadn't taken the time to learn it.

**Continue to be aware of the priorities
you are choosing.**

---

*. . . Build up, build up, prepare the way, remove every
obstruction from my people's way.*
Isaiah 57:14

Precious Present

Some days I feel like I can't wait until my baby is born so we can look into each other's eyes and do things together and hug each other. It will be so much fun to be a mother and to watch my child, instead of just feeling a little movement every once in a while.

Other days I think about the years John and I have had together before we thought about children. The long summer days of biking and gardening and cooling off in the river before coming home for a late supper are etched in my memory with beautiful and gentle strokes.

The days I treasure the most, however, are the ones when I live in the present with thanksgiving, rather than dream about history or my future. I am happy for memories and for plans, but I only have one chance at today's sunshine. The present is precious, and I'm in love.

**Let your soul be caressed
by the gentle awareness of God's presence
within you.**

---

*This is the day that the Lord has made;
let us rejoice and be glad in it.*
Psalm 118:24

Nausea's End

This evening I remembered that I didn't feel nauseated all day. When did this begin? I expected it to happen on the first day of my fourth month, the beginning of my second trimester, when the statistics say morning sickness subsides.

But it didn't stop that day, nor that week, and I was afraid I was going to be an abnormality who stayed sick for the entire pregnancy! I thought that I would be grateful every day for the rest of my life on every day when I was not nauseated, if that ever came to be. I wondered if all the people who aren't pregnant and aren't sick are appropriately grateful for their health.

Suddenly I realize that I have become one of those people. I don't know exactly when it happened. It's so easy to miss what isn't happening, and fail to be grateful when miserable things end.

**Thank you, God,
for helping me through the effects
of the first trimester.**

---

*Bless the Lord, O my soul,
and do not forget all his benefits.*
Psalm 103:2

Mother?

*E*very once in a while, like today, I get a panicky feeling. It twists my heart into my stomach and tells me I'm not going to be a good mother. What do I think I'm doing, bringing a baby into this world, into my family, into my house?

I don't have time for a child. I'm not patient enough. I don't like to work around other people's schedules—especially one that's going to be totally dependent on me for everything!

A few short months ago I was pleading to be able to give birth to a baby. Now I plead for a mother to be born in me.

**Give your questioning
to the One who created and nurtures you,
and will do the same for your child.**

*You hem me in,
behind and before,
and lay your hand upon me.*
Psalm 139:5

Awe

The fetal growth charts say that my baby now has all the parts a human being needs to survive, although not yet outside my uterus. It's hard to imagine that a human being is living inside me when my body hasn't noticeably changed a whole lot yet to prove a presence! How can such a tiny one be so fully alive?

I don't care how many women have experienced pregnancy before, or how often a child is born. My baby, inside me, is the most incredibly wonderful creation that has ever happened.

**Meditate on the intricacy
with which you and your baby
are created and joined.**

---

*I praise you,
for I am fearfully
and wonderfully made . . .*
Psalm 139:14

Baby's First Kick

Today I felt my baby moving for the first time. It was absolutely exciting! It was one of those moments that is so precious I wanted to hold it inside as my very own secret and have it announced to the world on the evening news, both at the same time!

I settled for telling everyone I saw or happened to dial on the phone. The woman checking out my groceries didn't seem to care a lot, but everyone else obliged me very kindly.

**God, there's really someone living inside me.
It seems too good to be true,
but I am ecstatic about it!**

---

*When Elizabeth heard Mary's greeting,
the child leaped in her womb . . .*
Luke 1:41

Communicating with Baby

ast night my husband told me he thought it was time to introduce himself to his baby. He put his face as close as he could to where we imagine the baby's ears might be and talked about how much he loves the tiny listener.

It does feel a little silly to talk to someone we can't see, but who knows how much this baby hears and feels and perceives from what we give? It's not hurting us, and it may be nurturing our baby, so who cares about a little silliness?

**No love
given to your unborn baby
is wasted.**

---

*For you shall go out in joy,
and be led back in peace . . .*
Isaiah 55:12

Pregnant Without the Effects!

After being consumed by the feelings and facts, excitement and exhaustion of pregnancy for almost four months, I'm suddenly in my fifth month and feel less pregnant than ever! Sometimes I forget that I am pregnant for most of a day. How can I forget that my body holds another person? But I do.

There's a cloud that has come to live over my head. I can't see it, but I feel it. It reminds me of the drastic changes that will soon shape my life. Sometimes it's a happy cloud that opens up to endless possibilities. Other times it has an air of enveloping doom about it. This month, however, I've rarely noticed the cloud. Life goes on as usual, and I wonder, sometimes, if I'm really pregnant.

**Be grateful
for the reprieve.**

*Seek the Lord and his strength;
seek his presence continually.*
Psalm 105:4

Second Trimester Energy

This must be the part I've heard about from the women who love being pregnant. I feel great! I no longer am consumed by nausea. My diet finally has grown beyond crackers and another kind of cracker. I can even cook again without getting sick.

My energy has returned, too—like a lost child, eager to make up for lost time. I have gained some weight, but I'm not big enough to restrict any activity I want to do. I finally have the energy to be thoroughly excited about being pregnant.

**Thank you, God,
for helping me along this journey
from daily survival to pure joy!**

---

*. . . your days of mourning
shall be ended.*
Isaiah 60:20

Protective

I've discovered yet another benefit of pregnancy. For the first time in my life I heard myself ask a stranger to put out his cigarette. I've never liked the smell, but I've often put up with it. Today, however, the protective mother in me watched that smoke zoom across the room, threatening to choke my baby. I decided not to let that happen.

He apologized at length, explaining that he hadn't noticed I was pregnant. That was simple! I wonder why I've never been able to do that for just me and my lungs.

**Let your baby's presence
empower you to do the loving thing
for yourself
that God, your parent,
would want for you.**

---

*The Lord is on my side
to help me . . .*
Psalm 118:7

Peace

I'm having another surge of the wonder of being pregnant, like I had when I first found out that I was. Now I can see that I'm pregnant! I'm not relying only on someone else's test and instruments. My body is showing me that there really is a baby in here.

This time, however, the joy is also more than a feeling. It's more like a companion. It seems like peace has been personified within and around me. Sometimes I even feel like this friend, Peace, carries me through my day so I don't hit the rough spots too hard. I've become oblivious to criticism and immune to feeling bad.

**Don't even think
about analyzing your peace;
just enjoy it.**

*How beautiful upon the mountains
are the feet of the messenger
who announces peace . . .*
Isaiah 52:7

*A*lone at last! This is unusual, for me to be excited about being alone. I must have gotten peopled-out this week.

Or maybe I'm starting to get more involved with the inward process of pregnancy. That makes it sound like pregnancy is a job, which I guess it is. I don't get paid for it, and I have to do it in conjunction with my other work, but in many ways it is a job.

John can help me do some of it, like becoming educated about the process of pregnancy, labor and delivery, and parenting. He can also help me relax. Nurturing a space for our baby to develop, however, is largely my own to do. I need time alone for the baby, to just be!

**Block out a little alone time each day
for your journey inward.**

---

*Be still and know that I am God!
I am exalted among the nations,
I am exalted in the earth.*
Psalm 46:10

Implosive

*J*ohn called in the middle of the day. Just hearing his voice, asking me how I'm doing, made me cry. I couldn't explain why. First of all I sobbed so hard I couldn't talk, and, secondly, I have no words for my feelings, at least none that make sense.

Yesterday the journey inward was entirely peaceful. Then today hit! I need my friends, but I don't act like it. I don't want to drive them away, so I explode into myself. The explosion breaks up into tears, which burst out as soon as there's an open door.

This turning inward with all my emotions feels unhealthy. It's so sudden, unexpected, and unfamiliar. I don't recognize myself.

Help me accept my new self, Lord.

Why are you cast down,
O my soul,
and why are you so disquieted within me?
Psalm 42:5

Stretch Marks

After I've faithfully rubbed cream on my growing belly for months, pinkish red, indented lines are beginning to appear all over the place! Now I find out that the most the cream ever did was keep me relaxed and smug in the knowledge that I was preventing stretch marks! What good is false knowledge?

It's one more unfamiliar sign that reminds me I'm pregnant, one more surprise for someone who generally likes to be more in control than I've felt lately, one more mark of the life within me.

True, I'm not planning to be in a bikini contest. Maybe I can convince myself to relish these lines as the royal marks of motherhood. They can help me remember that I will always need to practice stretching myself for this child.

**Let your skin
carry its story proudly.**

---

*If you direct your heart rightly,
you will stretch out your hands toward [God].*
Job 11:13

Unique Cry

9 was at a meeting last night where childcare was provided in the adjoining room for those who needed it. When I heard the babies cry I smiled to myself, happy to know they weren't my responsibility. It's nice to know that even though my baby cries sometimes, I don't have to listen to it yet. It made me appreciate again this time of silent development.

Then I noticed something strange. Every time a baby cried, one of the parents got up and went out. How did they know it was their baby? They all sound alike to me! What if I'm the first mother to not recognize her own baby's cry?

**Some motherly skills
are created at the moment of birth.**

---

*From this time forward
I make you hear new things,
hidden things that you have not known.*
Isaiah 48:6

Head and Heart

When I *think* about being pregnant, it seems like a blurringly busy time—shopping, reading, making doctor appointments, preparing the house, etc. When I pay attention to my *feelings* of being pregnant, however, time stands still. Busyness recedes until I'm left alone with just the two of us. I bow, awed by this experience of holding a life within me.

Both my thoughts and my feelings are vital to making the most of this time of pregnancy. I also need them both to prepare adequately for the future.

**Thank you, God,
for my head and my heart.**

---

*You shall love
the Lord your God with all your heart,
and with all your soul,
and with all your mind,
and with all your strength . . .
You shall love your neighbor as yourself . . .*
Mark 12:30,31

Babies Are Big

I went to visit a friend today whose baby was born just a week ago. I was amazed at how tiny the baby was. At six pounds, she was relatively small, so they say. Compared to the people I usually see, she was *definitely* small.

But then I was amazed to remember that six days ago, that entire baby was inside my friend! Now she suddenly looked huge.

Is my baby going to get that big before birth? Can my body accommodate all that life without bursting? I've watched it happen to other people, but it's still hard to believe this is happening to me.

Give your belly some tender, loving care, massaging it with a scented lotion.

Who has performed and done this,
calling the generations from the beginning?
I, the Lord, am first, and will be the last.
Isaiah 41:4

Waiting

Sometimes when I'm waiting I feel impatient and helpless. When I'm in a traffic jam with no escape route, or have already put all my groceries on the counter behind a person who can't find enough money to pay for his, I feel stuck. Screaming in my car might alleviate some tension, but in the supermarket I'd just be embarrassed by such childish behavior.

Today it's different. As I continue to wait for my baby's birth, I feel like I'm waiting in strength rather than passivity. Waiting doesn't seem idle or unproductive. I can almost feel the courage I will need for motherhood building up within me. Today I am strong in my waiting.

**Thank you, Lord,
for the times
when I can feel the strength of my waiting.**

*Wait for the Lord;
be strong,
and let your heart take courage;
wait for the Lord!*
Psalm 27:14

Boy or Girl?

When anyone asks me what sex I want my baby to be, I give the socially acceptable response, "It doesn't matter. I'm just hoping for a healthy baby." My husband speaks the same lack of preference.

When I'm daydreaming, though, I think about the fun of dressing a little girl and fixing her hair, of trading secrets about emerging womanhood, and of giggling together about "girl things."

I think my husband longs to share his maleness with a child of his own sex, too. He can relive the good memories of being a son with his father and create new ones he's had only in his dreams. I would enjoy watching him do that, too.

**Pray a blessing
on the father of your baby.**

*I will be a father to him,
and he shall be a son to me . . .*
II Samuel 7:14

Gratefulness

Sometimes I wonder what I did to deserve so much goodness in my life. I wonder why some people in this world suffer from starvation, war in their own towns, and incurable diseases, while it all seems far away from me.

I wonder how I've earned the privilege of working to pay for a home and furnishings, a car, and food. And now I have this—my very own child to love. How could anyone deserve a baby?

Then I remember that I've done nothing to deserve all these things. I become quietly aware of being connected to God and the world. My wonderings melt into a simple and deep gratefulness.

**Take nothing
for granted today.**

*Be exalted, O God,
above the heavens,
and let your glory be over all the earth.*
Psalm 108:5

Enchanted

Sometimes in the middle of my work, or while deciding which cereal to buy at the grocery store, I have this feeling that begins in my center and fans out to tingle all my senses. It says to me, "All is well."

I try to stay in that fantasy without naming it, like trying not to wake up from a good dream. I want to keep floating in that enchantment, and I'm afraid reality will destroy the mood.

When I remember, however, why that feeling has taken over my soul, the magic only surges. Oh yes, it's because I am pregnant!

**Live today as if you are enchanted.
Move as if you are floating.**

*Who can utter
the mighty doings of the Lord . . . ?*
Psalm 106:2

Celebration

I feel like a new person! I haven't felt this good for this long in four months. Actually, I've never felt this good since, before these four months began, I didn't know the joy of carrying a baby.

Now that I'm not too tired or sick to enjoy it, I feel like an ongoing celebration. Some days I want a loud celebration, one to talk about. I have to walk or run or find some other way to release my physical energy.

Today, though, my celebration is quiet and still. It's intense, but without words. I simply know that I'm a new person.

Celebrate life today.

You have turned my mourning into dancing;
you have taken off my sackcloth
and clothed me with joy.
Psalm 30:11

Maternal Glow

I saw a candle flickering inside a milky-colored lantern today, and I stopped to watch it. For some reason it caught my fascination more than an open flame that can be seen clearly. It held holiness and mystery.

Maybe my affinity for the shielded fire was its likeness to my own pregnant body. I often feel like I'm glowing from within. There are signs on the outside that a life flickers within me, but no one can see it clearly. There's only a hint of a deeper mystery, a holiness that demands respect. It's a God-lit space where creation continues, and I'm caught in the crossfire of love.

**Let the glow inside you
escape onto your face.**

*This is the Lord's doing;
it is marvelous in our eyes.*
Psalm 118:23

Mellowing

It was exquisitely pleasant to eat out with John last night for his birthday celebration. It wasn't profoundly wonderful or exciting. It was simply nice.

I was amazed by how satisfying it was to be alone with my husband. Ever since I can remember I've had a party on his birthday with lots of friends helping us celebrate. My parents tell me I've always loved being in crowds of friends. "The More We Get Together, the Happier We'll Be" is my theme song.

So this birthday was definitely different. But I'm reassured to know that I didn't feel pressure to have a big party, just because I usually do. If our friends feel left out, I'll blame my pregnancy. I can excuse anything with that these days!

**If you have mellowed,
respect yourself
above what others expect of you.**

---

*It is better to take refuge in the Lord
than to put confidence in princes.*
Psalm 118:9

See the Choices

I heard a woman from India talking this week about the huge birthday celebration they have in her home community when a member reaches 50 years of age. Fifty-year-olds are seen as ready to begin their careers. They have grown to maturity, raised their children, and are now ready to follow their individual interests.

If North American culture had those expectations, maybe I wouldn't feel the pressure to retain my career goals while in the middle of parenting. If 50 was our society's year of launching, rather than of winding down, I wouldn't fear that giving priority to motherhood might force me to lose the "golden years." If I don't try to do everything at the same time, maybe I can preserve my sanity and have a couple different sets of "golden years."

I don't have to let my society set my standards. It's easier to fit in, but not impossible to be different.

**Learn from your neighbors;
decide for yourself.**

---

*Happy are the people who know the festal shout,
who walk, O Lord,
in the light of your countenance.*
Psalm 89:15

Life Happens!

*L*ife seems so richly full. Today I need to plan for next week's workshop. I offered to be in charge of activities for our family reunion this summer. My work has given me the opportunity to be more creative than usual, and I've been thanked for what I've done. I'm excited about everything I'm doing these days.

The only thing that keeps developing, whether or not I work at it, however, is being pregnant. My baby keeps growing, even when I don't feel creative. My belly expands with no effort on my part.

Sometimes I attack life with energy. Now new energy is attacking me with life!

**In what part of your life
do you feel most fulfilled?**

---

*Come and see what God has done:
he is awesome in his deeds among mortals.*
Psalm 66:5

Joy Everywhere

I love days like today. Everywhere I go there is happiness. When I'm still, a holy hush falls around me. The maple leaves dance their trees to life. Pines sway to a tune only they can hear, but anyone who stops to notice can understand. Flowers are laughing and people join in.

My soul and body are setting forth ideal conditions for me to recognize the joy radiating from creation. Even though sometimes I still can't believe I'm pregnant, I'm sure I see joy everywhere because of what's growing in me!

**Recognize the joy
that flows back and forth between you
and the world.**

---

*The pastures of the wilderness overflow,
the hills gird themselves with joy,
the meadows clothe themselves with flocks,
the valleys deck themselves with grain,
they shout and sing together for joy.*
Psalm 65:12,13

My Mother

I've been thinking about my mother a lot lately. I remember her being at home all the time. Now that I've experienced the loneliness of coming home to an empty and silent house, void of supper smells at six in the evening, I know she gave me the stability a child needs without my ever realizing it.

Now I especially appreciate my mother. She read to me long after I could read to myself. She sang me to sleep at night and woke me with the smells of breakfast. She made clothes for my dolls. I'll never forget the summer afternoon she taught me how to make tambourines out of pop bottle lids on the back porch.

I remember a lot about my mother. I wonder what kind of child I was for her.

**Thank God for the woman
who gave life to you.**

---

*My child,
keep your father's commandment,
and do not forsake your mother's teaching.*
Proverbs 6:20

Mother Identity

I wonder if my mother will think I'm a good mother. I want her to, but I don't think I can do it like she did.

In many ways my life looks more like my dad's life. I have a job outside the home, and it's often supplemented by other projects, also away from home. I don't like to cook or clean any more than Dad did.

My mother never hired a babysitter so she could go to work. Dad, though, often went away on work-related trips for days at a time.

The Dad-part of me has been allowed to flourish so far in my life. Now the Mother-part is awakening, looking inward, nurturing, becoming non-competitive. I'm going to be a mother. I have to decide how my motherhood will look.

**Meditate on who your role models are
as you form your mother identity.**

---

*. . . you shall be happy,
and it shall go well with you.*
Psalm 128:2

Singing to Baby

*E*ven though babies are surrounded with fluid, I can't help but think they hear some of what goes on in the outside world. So I've been trying to remember to sing to my baby. If babies like to be comforted by their mothers' voices after they're born, it makes sense that they would find comfort in those sounds before they're born, too.

Singing has actually been self-nurturing as well. It reminds me to relax. It helps me to feel loved. It's also a good way to review the lullabies. I hadn't thought about them in years!

**Imagine God singing
a love song to you.**

. . . How good it is to sing . . .
Psalm 147:1

Big and Beautiful

"*Y*ou are beautiful."

I'm sure my husband didn't know how much I needed to hear those words today. Then again, maybe he did. Maybe that's why he said them.

Maybe he saw the scowl on my face as I looked into the mirror at my belly. This morning it no longer fit into my biggest, stretchiest skirt, and I just felt like a fat, unattractive blob. My face and hands look bloated. Even my hair is growing out of control, like the rest of me.

But another person's opinion can adjust my self-image in a heartbeat—especially when that person is someone I value. I couldn't take John with me, though, and I didn't get his remark on tape, so I couldn't replay it whenever I needed it. I'll have to put his comment deep inside me so I can hear it again when the blob-mentality threatens to take over again.

Thank you, God, for sending your love to me through my husband today.

The words of a whisperer are like delicious morsels; they go down into the inner parts of the body.
Proverbs 26:22

Always Hungry

few months ago, I hated the thought of food. Planning meals was worse than drudgery; it was repulsive. Grocery-shopping was tolerable if I did it when I wasn't nauseated, but it felt like wasted time. I wished I didn't have to eat. I wanted a break from the chore.

Now I'm eating whatever I see! Everything in the store looks wonderful. When my friends at work pack more than I think they need, I offer to help them out. I take seconds at every meal. Only occasionally do I remember to be embarrassed about my appetite.

Last night I went out with a friend who is pregnant. She ordered two glasses of water with her meal, because she was afraid the waitress wouldn't keep up with her needs. I laughed at her honesty, and the waitress did, too. Strangely enough, it's no joke! We pregnant women are constantly ravenous and parched.

Taking good care of your body and baby may not always be the most socially acceptable thing to do.

The sated appetite spurns honey,
but to a ravenous appetite even the bitter is sweet.
Proverbs 27:7

Food Dominates

can't believe I gained eight pounds in a month. I've been eating everything I could persuade others to give up, thinking all the time the baby was asking for it. But I know that the baby did not take on all eight of these pounds. Some of them will stay with me after the baby goes merrily on with life on the outside. I'll be left to contend with them on my own!

If I'm doomed to food preoccupation for several more months, I guess I'll study the pregnancy nutrition books and work on eating the right kinds of food. These recipes seem to have only half the sugar and salt I'm used to, but that should leave me with more room and available calories for the main meals. I can't seem to get my mind off eating en masse!

**All calories
were not created equal.**

---

*All things are lawful for me,
but not all things are beneficial . . .
Food is meant for the stomach
and the stomach for food . . .*
I Corinthians 6:12,13

Waddling

There is one thing I've been determined not to do. I will not waddle. I can't stop the front of me from sticking out, but I do not want the back of me flying out of control. I want to keep a dignified walk, at least.

I didn't know, though, that my hip joints would loosen. It's good mechanics, I guess, making labor and delivery easier for both of us. I just hadn't planned on losing some control over that part of what has held me together all these years.

I didn't have any concrete plans, I admit, about how to carry all this extra weight gracefully. I'm new at this, and turning to jelly in the process. I'm still learning how few choices I have to make about how to live through this pregnancy.

**Reserve your energy
for the things about which
you do have a choice.**

---

*. . . I will walk with integrity of heart
within my house.*
Psalm 101:2

Perpetual Spring

Outside, the seasons are changing again. For me the predictable signs of this time of year stabilize the world. Even though I am amazed by such changes four times a year, I can also rely on their regularity. I know what to expect.

I am glad to live within nature's gentle predictability, because inside me a new season is being born that I've never seen from this side before! Everything is different and changing, with no hint of the familiar. It's most like spring, but more than twice as long. I feel connected to all the earth: reproducing like living things are created to do, glorifying the One who created us, and thus receiving the gift of renewed life myself.

With which season do you most identify at this point in your pregnancy?

Is there a thing of which it is said,
"See, this is new"?
It has already been, in the ages before us.
Ecclesiastes 1:10

Vision

I was just re-reading my journal from a year ago, and I had to laugh. I had made a list of the things I was praying about. There were a lot of either-or kinds of things: "God, help me decide whether I should do this or that."

The funny part is that when I became pregnant soon thereafter, I suddenly had a whole new set of matters to pray about. Some of my prayers have been answered in ways I hadn't ever considered. Other requests became obsolete.

It makes me wonder about my current thinking and praying. What blinders am I wearing that keep me from seeing all the possibilities? I probably have more choices than I realize. I'm glad I'm not the only one in charge of my life.

**Ask for an expansion
of your vision.**

---

*By day the Lord commands his steadfast love,
and at night his song is with me,
a prayer to the God of my life.*
Psalm 42:8

Blessings

The morning is cool, the bike ride was invigorating, the hot tea is wonderful, the night was too short, it's energizing to have some quiet time to think and write, it's very good to be pregnant. Sometimes I think heaven can't be any better than this, except maybe the prospect of never being tired.

My thoughts are scattered all over my life, remembering the past, reaching into the future, enjoying today. For once I feel no need to gather my thoughts together. I love being surrounded by goodness. The farther I stretch to notice, the more engulfed I become in my blessings.

**Meditate
on the goodness
of your life.**

*You have multiplied,
O Lord my God,
your wondrous deeds
and your thoughts toward us . . .*
Psalm 40:5

Their Rain Can't Get In

Today one of my friends was upset about three or four bad things that have happened to her. I did a really poor job of being sympathetic. This second trimester bliss has so taken over my mood that I just couldn't let her struggles move in on me. I felt like I was reading a sad book, rather than listening to the real details of my friend's life. When she left, I offered a prayer for her well-being, closed the book, and went on noticing my quiet joy.

I hope she doesn't think I don't care. On the other hand, I'm glad to have this break from feeling so burdened by other's problems and letting their pain inside me.

**Nurture your joy
without feeling guilty about those
for whom you aren't offering care right now.**

---

*My heart is steadfast, O God,
my heart is steadfast . . .*
Psalm 108:1

Pregnancy Holds

When I worked with troubled girls I was continually amazed by how faithfully many of them loved their mothers. Even mothers who neglected, abused, and repeatedly broke promises could not squelch their daughters' longing to be accepted and loved by them. After all, that's what mothers are supposed to do, isn't it? The girls were sure there were reasons their mothers appeared to be uncaring, even if they didn't know what they were. Making derogatory comments about someone else's mother was cause for an instant fight.

That strong bond of hope makes more sense to me now that I'm pregnant. These girls had within them the subconscious memory of being held in the most intimate of ways, which is deeper than reason. In their beginnings they received months of constant touch. No one could take away from them the fact that each had been carried by her own. Each belonged to a particular woman.

**Thank you, God, for giving everyone
a beginning of being held;
thank you for creating me with a capacity to hold.**

Tell the innocent how fortunate they are . . .
Isaiah 3:10

Overriding Love

I can't conceive of abandoning or abusing my child like the mothers of the troubled girls I worked with. But those daughters' undying love for their mothers gives me the assurance I need right now.

I think a lot about the teenagers I've seen who turn against their parents—ignore their values, blatantly disobey, and talk hatefully to them. It makes me wonder how I could bear having a child do that to me, a child whom I already love so deeply, a child to whom I will give much more by the time we hit the teenage years together.

The strength of the mother-child bond, no matter what mistakes I make, gives me hope. We will likely hurt each other, but we will, most certainly, love each other.

It's not too early to pray for the years ahead when your baby will be a teenager.

May our sons in their youth
be like plants full grown,
our daughters like corner pillars,
cut for the building of a palace.
Psalm 144:12

Home Will Happen

My child will be a city child! That was a strange thought, bursting out of my peace like a volcano. I've lived in the city for 10 years now, and I've come to love its diversity and opportunity.

When I was a child I lived in the country. I ran free in the meadow, explored in the creeks, and rode my horse for miles through the woods. What will my child do in the city? Do children and cities go together?

My brother assumes we will move to the country now that I'm pregnant. That would be easy in some ways; it would be a more familiar way for me to raise a child. I've found home here, though, and I believe my child will find home wherever I'm able to help create it.

You, more than your environment, will determine what kind of home your child is born into.

---

*. . . the Lord declares to you
that the Lord will make you a house.*
II Samuel 7:11

Friends Forever?

After my baby is born, what will happen to my friendships with those friends who don't have children? I know I will still need them to talk to me about world news and the meaning of life! My friends who have recently become parents seem to talk to me only about diapers, doctors, and feeding schedules.

Soon I will need my friends without children more than ever. It will likely be late at night when I will get the urge to socialize—after my baby is asleep—so they will need to come to *my* house for tea! My friends with children will be stuck in their own homes, too. And a phone call just doesn't do the trick when it's a mood I want to share.

What will I have to offer these friends without children? Will they still need me, too? I worry about it. I'll just have to wait and see about some things.

**Nurture
the friendships you value.**

---

*Do not let loyalty and faithfulness forsake you;
bind them around your neck,
write them on the tablet of your heart.*
Proverbs 3:3

Making Love

During the first four months I was pregnant, sex seemed like a bad word. I was nauseated, forever tired, and trying to get used to all the changing feelings happening inside. I simply wanted to be alone with my body. Actually, I didn't always want to be in it myself!

"Sex" still does not seem like the right word. "Making love" seems more appropriate. My body is my friend again and is also ready to befriend my husband! All these physical and emotional changes keep my head spinning. I won't analyze this one, though. I'll just enjoy it while it lasts!

**"Normal" is still whatever
is right for you.**

---

*O my dove, in the clefts of the rock . . .
let me see your face,
let me hear your voice;
for your voice is sweet,
and your
face is lovely.*
Song of Solomon 2:14

Questions

Will my baby really care enough about the softness of a cloth diaper to make it worth the extra bother? Will the environment suffer significantly if it has to deal with only one more child's disposables? Will my baby be so much healthier with breast milk, than a commercial formula, that it will be worth the discipline of either pumping or always being available? Will my baby enjoy the stimulus of being with lots of other babies and adults that a childcare center provides, or is the consistency of home care invaluable?

So many questions hang around to be answered, getting louder as the months go by. Plenty of people have answers, but they are only theirs. We have to come up with ours by ourselves—our own family.

**Almighty God,
lend me a drop of your wisdom.**

*. . . wisdom will come into your heart,
and knowledge will be pleasant to your soul.*
Proverbs 2:10

Worried

When I think about all the questions for which I need to find answers, all the decisions I must make about my baby's needs, I realize there's one uncertainty that stays stuck way in the bottom. It hurts when I acknowledge it, like a lump that my stomach can't digest. I try to ignore it, but it keeps bumping around. Sometimes I worry so much I get a headache. Saying it aloud would give it too much power, and then it might engulf my sanity. Furthermore, I don't want to hear anyone's response, which would certainly be, "Oh, don't worry about *that!*"

If I could help it, of course I wouldn't worry, but the question gnaws away at my innards and so I hear it. I just want to know if my baby is healthy.

**Give your worries
to One who is greater than you
and more capable of carrying them.**

*O Lord,
you will ordain peace for us . . .*
Isaiah 26:12

Earth Mother

As I was watering the garden today, I remembered my doctor's advice. She told me to keep drinking lots of water.

Suddenly I felt a deep connection with the earth and with the One who nourishes both of us with new life. My baby demands the care and attention that would always be good for my body, but which I find harder to give it when I'm not affecting anyone else. Now I am affecting someone else, and it's up to me to keep watering this garden!

**Imagine that you are a flower,
soaking up the cool water
of the One who is creating life
in you.**

*You visit the earth and water it,
you greatly enrich it;
the river of God is full of water . . .*
Psalm 65:9

Interruptions

A friend with a newborn came over last night for supper. I realize now that I should appreciate the lack of interruptions in my current dining routine, and in life in general!

She was continually jumping up from the table to comfort her baby, change his diaper, give him toys to look at, and talk to him. We never had a single complete conversation! My friend didn't have a chance at a second helping of the main course—we were waiting for dessert long before she finished her salad.

Maybe that's how mothers lose their weight from pregnancy.

**Know that you will have
the energy it takes
to mother your baby
as you simultaneously
are comforted by your divine Parent.**

*As a mother comforts her child,
so I will comfort you . . .*
Isaiah 66:13

Nursing

Something else happened with my dinner guest and her newborn last night. After supper she disappeared for half an hour to nurse her baby. I guess she didn't feel comfortable doing it in front of us.

I've always assumed I would breast-feed my baby, too, since it's cheaper, it's healthier, and my mother did it! But I'm not sure I'm willing to give up socializing while I do it. I can't stand to hear people talking and laughing without being a part of it. One more thing to think about!

**Plan ahead—
the how, when, and where of feeding times—
so you feel at ease with your decision.**

---

*. . . that you may nurse and be satisfied
from her consoling breast . . .*
Isaiah 66:11

Unique

From my kitchen window, on occasion, I see a white squirrel scamper up and down the trees. I always stop what I'm doing and watch with fascination when he comes into sight, not because he acts any differently than any other squirrel, but because his unique color makes him stand out. Elmo, as the neighborhood children have named him, is a freak of nature.

I wonder how I'll react if something in my baby's appearance is unusually different from other babies. Will I be embarrassed, or will I be able to see the unique beauty? Even if my baby looks normal, he's bound to behave in ways I wish he wouldn't. I'll have to choose whether to let that embarrass me or to show me the beauty of my child's uniqueness!

**Pray that you can accept
the uniqueness your baby
will undoubtedly provide to the world.**

---

*May the Lord give strength to his people!
May the Lord bless his people with peace!*
Psalm 29:11

Thermos

*J*ohn says that after eight years of marriage, he feels like he's sleeping with another woman. He used to beg me to wear socks to bed to melt the ice around my toes. This new woman's feet warm his! He used to have to fight for the covers. This new woman flings the covers over onto him to break her sweat.

I'm trying to relearn the appropriate way to dress. I feel like before I begin to dress I already have a layer of thermal underwear hugging my skin. I dress the way my brain generally directs for this weather, and by breakfast I'm sweating. I dread the coming of summer!

**Concentrate today
on enjoying one of the new aspects
of being a pregnant woman.**

---

*A new heart I will give you,
and a new spirit I will put within you . . .*
Ezekiel 36:26

Becoming

$\mathcal{I}$s it possible that my child can help me maintain an attitude of love rather than judgment? Babies are symbols of love. It's hard not to love them! Even when they cause pain, it's not their fault. Because they are dependent, they give unconditional love to their caretakers. They receive love as freely as they give it. I'm hoping my baby will remind me regularly of the beauty of love.

On the other hand, I'm most vulnerable to harboring negative thoughts when I'm tired. Having this baby will certainly increase the risk on that front. In the end, I can't count on a baby to make the ugly parts of my personality go away. I'll enjoy those times when our bond of love makes me a better person. I'll keep working on the job of becoming, the rest of the time.

**Help me, God,
to not expect too much from my baby.**

---

*[Love] bears all things,
believes all things,
hopes all things,
endures all things.*
I Corinthians 13:7

Quality Time

"It's not the amount of time you spend with your child that matters, but the way you spend the time when you are together." That's the advice I've been hearing and reading. Quality is more important than quantity.

I understand how that is true to some extent. If I'm always at home with my child, but constantly trying to take care of my responsibilities, my child might have more fun playing with other children, at least part of the time. Then I could be more available when we are together. On the other hand, children need to learn how to play alone, too.

No one else's answers will work for me. I'll have to find my own balance after my baby's personality emerges and mingles with mine!

**Accepting the quality of God's love
will help to shape the quality
you have to give.**

---

*. . . I have loved you with an everlasting love;
therefore I have continued my faithfulness to you.*
Jeremiah 31:3

Puzzle of Time

Sometimes I wish someone could just give me the answers, pure and simple. "The healthiest child is the one who spends 20 hours in day care building social skills, 10 hours at home playing alone, and two hours each day of quality time with at least one parent" . . . or something like that. I'd be willing to figure out a way to give my child what is best, if I just knew what that was.

My baby is a human being, the same as I am. My baby will have a unique personality and needs. That's the challenging part of the puzzle. I can't see the finished product now, but I'm blessed to be given the chance to help fit the pieces together.

Trust that God will continue to guide you in wisdom.

The fear of the Lord is the beginning of wisdom . .
Psalm 111:10

Alone?

We were off to a vacation at the beach! I had waited a long time for this week—the last vacation my husband and I would spend alone, together, for a long time.

We talked little on the drive down as we let go of the busyness that led up to our time away. We relished the silence that we guessed future vacations would lack.

That night as I snuggled up as close as my stomach would let me get to him, I was surprised to hear a disappointed voice. "I thought this was just going to be the two of us," he said.

**Make good use of the time you have left,
when you won't be interrupted
by the cries of your baby.**

---

*. . . Arise, my love,
my fair one, and come away.*
Song of Solomon 2:13

Change

$\mathcal{J}$ couldn't wait to get to the sand. I dug a hole the size of my belly and lined it with my beach towel. It was my only chance to lie on my belly for at least three months to come. I could act like it was just me in this body again!

I slowly sank into the sand cradle, only to realize I had to dig two more holes just above the first one if I really wanted to be comfortable. I forgot that part of me was growing, too! I'm being continually reminded that the changes for which I plan will be accompanied by changes I hadn't anticipated.

**What are the changes your pregnancy
has brought?**

For everything there is a season . . .
Ecclesiastes 3:1

Focused

The ocean gloriously echoes the wonder of pregnancy and life. The ebb and flow of the waves, that constant promise of the sea, remind me that I'm not in control of life. Someone much greater than I am has made all I see and experience. It makes sense to commit this new little life to that One.

The roar of the waves drowns out many other voices and matters of importance for me these few days. I am able to remember how few things are really important. I hope this focus lasts long enough for me to take it back into my everyday world, always remembering how significant it is for me to be part of creating a baby.

Imagine lying on a warm beach.
Listen to the waves
and let them drown out all
but the most important things
you need to hear today.

. . . And be thankful.
Let the word of Christ dwell in you richly . . .
Colossians 3:15-16

Staying Centered

This summer the mosquitoes are insufferable at the ocean—whenever I walk away from the waves. I am extremely annoyed! My favorite place, both for respite from the mosquitoes, as well as the peaceful rhythm of the surf, is being as close to the water as I can get. Fear of the tides keeps me from sleeping on the beach at night, but I can spend my entire day there—eating, reading, playing, napping.

This is all emerging for me as a symbol of God's fearful awesomeness, combined with God's protective love. Whether I'm always conscious of the winds of God in my life or not, I intend to stay close to where the waves are so that I can know peace.

**Imagine God's protective love,
blowing away an annoyance
that is making your life miserable right now.**

*. . . let the peace of Christ
rule in your hearts . . .*
Colossians 3:15

Denial

$\mathcal{E}$pidural, perineum, kegels, sitz baths, breech, Pitocin, etc., etc. There are too many strange and awful-sounding terms flying around. I don't want to read anything else. My peace and sanity are threatened by all these things I'm supposed to be thinking about, deciding, learning.

I have no desire or energy left to decide anything! Let me please just curl up in a womb somewhere, float around in the calm waters of love, and have someone else do all the worrying for me. This sofa and blanket and pillow will do very well . . .

**Denial
is sometimes
an appropriate coping mechanism.**

---

*Come . . . enter your chambers,
and shut your doors behind you;
hide yourselves for a little while . . .*
Isaiah 26:20

Imagine!

It's hard to imagine that God cares about every person in every car I pass on the road, as much as I believe God cares about me. It's hard to imagine that God cares about everyone's babies in the whole world as much as I know God cares about mine. It's hard to imagine that God accompanies every woman in her pregnancy with all the emotional ups and downs, as much as I've felt God's presence in my roller-coaster life these past six months.

Maybe that's just part of being human—having a hard time imagining divine omnipresence. I'm thankful that even if I wasn't given understanding, at least I was given the ability to trust.

**Thank you, God,
for caring about me and my baby,
in spite of all the other women
and babies there are for you to care about, too.**

---

*O Lord, you have searched me and known me.
You know when I sit down and when I rise up;
you discern my thoughts from far away.*
Psalm 139:1,2

Satisfaction

There's a point in every holiday meal when I could stop eating and feel completely satisfied. It comes somewhere between tasting a little of each delicacy and the middle of dessert. Unfortunately, I usually don't stop soon enough, and I end up feeling stuffed rather than comfortably satisfied.

At this point in my pregnancy, I feel like I am at that wonderfully pleasurable moment—my whole being, mind, and body is full of blissful, deep, overwhelming satisfaction. I want to sit here for five more minutes, breathing deeply of this precious moment. This time I don't have a choice about whether or not to keep going. I will, no doubt, soon feel stuffed!

**Think of your life as a meal.
What part are you enjoying today?**

My soul is satisfied as with a rich feast . . .
Psalm 63:5

Free Time

$\mathcal{I}$ gave in to my compulsive streak today and made a chart of my weekly schedule. I even color-coded it. My favorite color, yellow, shows my free time. I did all this because, with all the many demands on my time, I was sure I had no more free time. I still wish there were more yellow spaces, but at least I can now see that I do have time every day when I can choose what to do.

The next step, after recognizing my free time, is to learn to enjoy it. I've been so busy grieving the time when I can't choose what I do, that I haven't appreciated enough when I can spend it freely.

Be thankful for every moment of freedom when you can choose how to use your time.

Out of my distress I called on the Lord;
the Lord answered me
and set me in a broad place.
Psalm 118:5

Good-Bye Stress

So now that I realize I do have some freedom in my days, how should I responsibly use those times? I've just made a list of ways I can enjoy those moments of choice. I will intentionally relax a little bit every day and let go of the stress. If I don't, and unconsciously hold onto the stress, my muscles will be more sore than necessary.

Here is part of my coping plan: listen to music, roll my head and shoulder muscles, write in my journal, go for a walk, eat a doughnut (don't tell my doctor), and play the piano. I don't need long periods of time. Just thinking of the options already makes me feel less controlled by my schedule.

**What relaxation triggers
can you fit into your moments of free choice?**

*From the rising of the sun to its setting
the name of the Lord is to be praised.*
Psalm 113:3

Womb of God

*L*ast weekend I visited a friend in West Virginia. We took long hikes through her striking playground—the "hollers" where I felt surrounded by peace and safety. In the mountains I sensed freedom to wander within majestic security. The blue sky covered me as gently as the moss held me.

I reflected on the similarities between what I was experiencing and how my baby experiences life so far. This is the only period of life when I will be able to completely surround my baby. I love it! I am an agent of freedom within walls of safety and security.

I lived in the West Virginia womb of God for a weekend. I am renewed with love and rich in the promise of eternal peace.

**Think of your favorite place in the world.
Go there in your imagination
and let God hold you there in peace.**

---

*As the mountains surround Jerusalem,
so the Lord surrounds his people,
from this time on and forevermore.*
Psalm 125:2

Advice:
Unsolicited and Unappreciated

One of the women I work with told me today that she's concerned about me. I'm not spending enough energy on preparing myself for this baby. I'm emotionally disconnected, she said.

Maybe she's right—at least partly. I'm not sure, though, how to do any more. My schedule is still my own, so I keep it full. There's no one crying for supper, so I often work late. No one complains about not having sufficient milk, so I forget to drink enough liquids. I don't know how to talk about a baby I haven't seen yet, so I talk about other things.

That woman isn't one of the people I would confide in anyway. I think, after considering her unsolicited advice, I'll keep living life my own way, since it is mine.

**Be open to the advice of others,
but don't let it drown out your inner voice.**

---

*Like a sparrow in its flitting,
like a swallow in its flying,
an undeserved curse goes nowhere.*
Proverbs 26:2

Hiccups

This is the funniest thing—now that I know what's happening! At first when I felt those short jerky movements, I was scared. It wasn't the same as kicking. I thought my baby was having convulsions.

When I learned that, even in the womb, babies get hiccups, I knew that's what I'd been feeling. Supposedly it's not uncomfortable for the baby, so I will just enjoy this reminder of life. Now if we could restrict the hiccups to when I'm not trying to sleep, I would find it a whole lot funnier!

**Already I cannot control my baby,
but at least it's funny!**

---

*Then our mouth was filled with laughter,
and our tongue with shouts of joy;
then it was said among the nations,
"The Lord has done great things for them."*
Psalm 126:2

Attention, Please!

$\mathcal{I}$f I thought hiccups were entertaining, tonight's drama was twice as good. As far as I could tell, my baby was sleeping and I was heading in that direction myself. I was curled up in the corner of a big chair—well, as curled up as I can get these days! I had propped a book up on my belly, thinking it was good to have some use for this growing pillow, when, suddenly, the book went flying right out of my hands.

That was one powerful kick! This little tyke is already vying for my attention!

Recognize new forms of entertainment as your life becomes more sedentary.

Great are the works of the Lord, studied by all who delight in them.
Psalm 111:2

Gentleness

*A*ll of life seems gentle today. Nothing special is happening. In fact, it's the simple beauty of the ordinary which has come alive with gentleness.

My baby moves gently within me, like he's amused with twiddling his fingers or learning how to float on his back. My belly has grown to a gentle size, swollen into a neatly transportable package that speaks of stability and surprise at the same time. The wind is caught up in the gentleness of the season, as well, and carries the rich smells of earth to me.

I think I even have the energy to create the gentle smell of bread in my home. This second trimester is certainly a gift. I am in love with life—in a gentle way, of course.

**Give yourself time to relax
into the gentleness of being pregnant.**

---

*Faithfulness will spring up from the ground,
and righteousness will look down from the sky.
The Lord will give what is good . . .*
Psalm 85:11,12

Satisfied

Today I picked up a friend from the pre-school where she works. While I waited for her, I watched a three-year-old paint a picture. First she made a few deliberate lines. Then she carefully filled them in until a solid circle appeared. Then she picked up another brush with another color of paint and painted with both hands, flowing in all directions at the same time. When every inch of the paper was covered with the same brownish color, she put the brushes down with a sigh of satisfaction and ran off to play with the blocks.

That's kind of how I feel I'm working at being me these days. I'm creating someone else. We're getting all blended together. I can no longer see what was here to begin with, nor make clear distinctions about what is who now, but I feel richly satisfied.

**What colors is your life painting
with your baby today?**

*He himself is before all things,
and in him all things hold together.*
Colossians 1:17

Secret

My husband thinks I can't keep a secret. That might be true most of the time, but now I feel like I'm living a secret. I'm not trying to keep something from others, as much as keep it for myself. I'm afraid that if I try to put the secret into words, it will be ruined.

This secret doesn't have words. Others know I'm pregnant, but that's not the whole secret. John knows my feelings and thoughts better than anyone, but I don't try to explain the secret to him. I don't want to diminish the secret by confining it to even the most eloquent language. I just have to let it be mine.

**Treat yourself to time alone
to enjoy your wordless secret.**

. . . [God] knows the secrets of the heart.
Psalm 44:21

Co-Dependence

I have this due date. The doctor calls it my due date, anyway. So do the charts. We all know we can't count on it as the birth day of my baby, but I've made appointments for myself right up to that date, and I have plans for after it, as if I know exactly when it will happen.

It's strange to know that my baby, tiny and unseen, already has the power to determine my schedule and keep me unsettled with guessing, to hold me all the time unaware. We are caught in a web of dependency on each other.

Revel in the mysterious secret your child and body hold from you.

Think of us in this way,
as servants of Christ
and stewards of God's mysteries.
I Corinthians 4:1

Partners in Growth

I was totally engrossed in a seminar at work today, trying to grasp the concepts and how they will fit into my work. Suddenly a swift kick in the ribs made me sit back and smile. For a moment I was oblivious to anyone else, and then, just as quickly, I was smug in my little secret about the partner I had brought along.

My baby's reminder of life produced paradoxical feelings. With that kick, nothing else seemed important except my baby and me. What I was learning and being trained to become slid back in significance.

On the other hand, all of life became of utmost importance. I want to keep growing and learning and working at being the best person I can possibly be. I'm helping my baby to grow. How can I give myself any less? We will grow together.

**You can give to your baby
by giving to yourself.**

---

*I will look with favor on the faithful in the land,
so that they may live with me . . .*
Psalm 101:6

Nightmares

I woke up this morning, not knowing for a few foggy moments if I was dreaming, or if I really did have a baby with Downes Syndrome. One attempt to turn over told me that the baby was still tucked right in under my ribs!

Last week I dreamed that a visiting nurse came by after the baby was born to make sure I knew what I was doing. I went to the oven and showed her I had put the baby there to keep her warm. Only then did I realize what a terrible thing I had done.

I've tried not to let fears of my inadequacy or the baby's possible imperfections enter my thoughts, so maybe that's why they're coming alive in my dreams. I've heard pregnancy nightmares are normal; I could sleep better if I weren't so normal.

**Allow your nightmares
to enlighten you about the inner workings
of your soul.**

---

*The secret things belong to the Lord our God,
but the revealed things belong to us
and to our children forever.*
Deuteronomy 29:29

Child Abuse

I have never liked to think about children being abused. Most people would probably understand that sense of horror. The closer I get to seeing my baby face to face, however, the more fanatical I feel about the subject. How could anyone mistreat a little, innocent, helpless baby?

Suddenly, child abuse is more than something with which I logically disagree. It's a feeling of sickening disgust that starts in my stomach and spreads with heat into the rest of me. I still want to be a social worker, but don't let me near parents who abuse their children. I can't think rationally, right now, about their point of view.

**Pray for patience
for what lies ahead.**

Love is patient; love is kind . . .
I Corinthian 13:4

Morning Thanks

This morning I woke up between 4:30 and 5:00. By 6:00 I was so uptight about not being able to go back to sleep, that it was worthless to keep trying.

Thinking that this early morning wake-up might be preparation for what lies ahead, I decided to make the most of it. I almost had fun. I convinced myself that it was an adventure to be the first one awake and have time to myself before the demands of the day began. The morning was loud with waking-up noises—birds and traffic—but none of it was my noise. I had time to just be and enjoy my inner silence.

It turned out to be a wonderful morning. I had time to give thanks for my life.

**Let your frustration
about wakeful times at night
be turned into prayer.**

---

*Awake my soul! . . .
I will awake the dawn.
I will give thanks to you, O Lord . . .*
Psalm 108:1-3

Horror Stories

Why do people have to tell their worst labor-and-delivery stories around me? A pregnant woman entering a room must trigger the reflex that stirs horrid memories and leaves people helpless to keep their thoughts to themselves.

Today one of my co-workers stopped herself in the middle of a story about her best friend almost dying from an epidural to tell me not to listen. Not listen!?

And all this was apparently in response to someone asking me how I am doing. I had said I'm getting nervous about labor and delivery. This colleague of mine has obviously never been pregnant.

I think I need some new friends.

**Balance out the horror stories
you inevitably hear
with stories of joy.**

---

*Remember the wonderful works [the Lord] has done,
his miracles, and the judgments he uttered,
O offspring of his servant Abraham . . .
his chosen ones.*
Psalm 105:5,6

Alien

Sometimes I feel like a resident alien. This is my home, but none of my relatives live here, at least not close enough to be potential babysitters! Many of my values are different from the people I work with and even from some of my best friends. John and I drive an ancient pickup truck instead of a modern mini-van. I spend my free time differently than most people, and I seem to vote for the losing candidate more often than not.

I didn't even get pregnant when many of my peers were starting their families. Now all they have to offer me is sympathy for the impending loads of laundry and loss of sleep—no camaraderie.

Some days the uniqueness of my life energizes me. Other days, the loneliness of being an alien gnaws at my heart. Yet on either kind of day, the increasing strength of my inner kicker reminds me that life will be manageable. We are at home with each other.

**Spend some time today
celebrating your unique beauty.**

*. . . Jacob lived as an alien in the land of Ham.
And the Lord made his people very fruitful.*
Psalm 105:23,24

Forgetfulness

$\mathcal{I}$ can't believe I forgot my doctor's appointment! It's written right there on my calendar, but I forgot to look at that, too. I've been forgetting a lot of things lately. I feel like I'm losing control of myself when I can't remember the promises I make to people.

When I complained about this to a friend, she said, "You must be pregnant or something." So this is another part of pregnancy!

It doesn't make sense to me, but I guess I'll milk it while I have an excuse for being irresponsible! Maybe I'll forget my dentist appointment tomorrow, too.

**Be glad your worth
does not depend on your reliability.**

---

*. . . All people are grass,
their constancy is like the flower of the field . . .
The grass withers, the flower fades;
but the word of our God will stand forever.*
Isaiah 40:6,8

Mobile Home

*E*very time I go past a mirror and see my belly, I laugh. It's me, and yet it's not! I still don't expect to see that much of me.

It's fun to be different for a season. It's fun to have new clothes and to feel like a mobile home for this tiny bundle who snuggles up inside of me. "Cozy" doesn't seem a fitting word for a body that expands by the day, and yet that's exactly who we are together—a big ball of cozy.

**Pray peace into the expanding home
you embody.**

. . . Blessed is the womb that bore you . . .
Luke 11:27

Good-Bye Singleness

$\mathcal{I}$ thought I said good-bye to singleness on my wedding day. I was no longer alone. I no longer made my own plans about whom to be with and what to do every Friday night. I had companionship and twice as many ideas of things to do and places to go. But I consulted with someone else now, instead of making spontaneous plans with my other friends. I was free to make many of my own choices, but now I called home if I was going to be late.

Now that I'm about to be a mother, however, I see John and me as two adults, committed and single at the same time. The weight of responsibility for a dependent baby approaches and makes me feel like I'm giving up my freedom. Parenthood does not sound nearly as "single" as marriage has been.

**Every new stage of life
calls for giving up at least part
of the prior stage.**

. . . a time to mourn and a time to dance.
Ecclesiastes 3:4

Inner Conflict

When I complained about my backaches to a friend, she promptly copied pages from a book of exercises to help relieve back pain in pregnant women. That was kind of her; it's even kinder that she's never asked me how I'm doing with those exercises. I tried to do a couple of them, but they just took too much energy and I went to bed instead.

I keep those pages exposed on my reading pile, hoping that I'll be inspired, but somehow it just doesn't happen. I'm so consumed with enduring pregnancy and preparing for childbirth that every day ends with more ideas of things to do than I've yet done. I feel like a spoiled kid. I just want the pain to disappear without having to do anything. I hate being lazy . . . and yet, here I sit! Maybe I just hate the *thought* of being lazy.

**Let your inner conflict enlighten you
about who you are,
without thinking any less of yourself as a person.**

---

*I do not understand my own actions.
For I do not do what I want,
but I do the very thing I hate.*
Romans 7:15

Choosing a Name

On Jesus' day, a Jewish baby wasn't given a name until the eighth day of life. In some countries today where infant mortality is high, a baby is often not named for the first year. Nonetheless, I would like to have a name picked out for my baby before I give birth.

I've looked through piles of name books and in the "New Arrivals" section of the newspaper. Nothing seems perfect enough for my child. Even when I like a name, I wonder if I'll get tired of it. A name is a big responsibility to take on for another person.

Giving this child a name, however, becomes an opportunity to bless it, also. I can pass on identity and create a welcome to humanity. What a gift to have the job of naming this child!

**Choose a meaningful name with care,
and then know your love for the name
will grow with your love for your child.**

. . . your name endures to all generations.
Psalm 102:12

Absentminded

What I thought was going to be a blissful day off, all to myself, has turned into a nightmare. I spent two hours looking for the keys to the neighbors' house. I promised to feed their dog for the next three days while they're out of town. The small inconvenience has just grown immensely with my newfound ability to forget everything! I'm afraid I'm facing a looming disability.

I know the dog won't starve to death in three days, but she's probably in there wetting their Persian rugs this very minute. I wonder if it's more expensive to fix a broken window or hire a locksmith to break in.

I'll soon have to find another source of income to support the symptoms of my pregnancy. I should be able to get a tax deduction for being pregnant.

**Forgive yourself and forget it,
no matter how much it costs.**

---

*. . . as far as the east is from the west,
so far [the Lord] removes our transgressions from us.*
Psalm 103:12

Growth Spurt

When I attempted my usual pop-out-of-bed-with-the-alarm action this morning, I didn't make it! I believe I gained 10 pounds overnight, all of it in my middle. The ease with which I am used to slipping in and out of bed, on and off chairs, and in and out of cars has suddenly come to a halt. I've had to start adding a roll to boost the momentum.

I was noticing the inconvenience of my pregnancy more than ever as I left the house today. Then I met a woman who asked about my due date. When I said it's in two months, she said, "Oh, you don't look that pregnant!" I decided to make her my new best friend.

**Give thanks for the people
God sends in and out of your life.**

---

*Answer me when I call,
O God of my right!
You gave me room when I was in distress . . .*
Psalm 4:1

Premature

Four months ago I left behind most of my conscious worries about miscarrying. Yet I find that I am relieved because if my baby were to be born now, its chances of survival would be good. I don't want it to happen, but I know our hospital has a whole room full of babies whose mothers had to go home long before the infants were released.

It must be upsetting to give birth prematurely. If my baby were born this month, nothing would be ready—my home, my head, or my heart. It would be a harsh reversal of my dreams and plans about how it's "supposed" to be.

I am still less anxious, knowing that my baby could be kept alive in the case of some emergency. It's one more miracle of life.

**Thank God
for the safety your baby grows into daily.**

*I declare that your steadfast love is established forever;
your faithfulness is as firm as the heavens.*
Psalm 89:2

Individuality of Baby

What fun! Tonight as our growing family was resting on the couch, our baby started playing with us. Every time we touched my belly, we got a punch back from the other side. Once, when we hadn't "played back" for a few minutes, the baby jumped all the way across from one side of me to the other.

What a strange, incredible, exciting feeling to have life within me. I've known it's there, but suddenly it's more than just a part of me. It's another life, responding to me, rather than with me.

**Pray for the grace
to allow your baby to be an individual,
rather than merely an extension of you.**

---

*. . . as soon as I heard the sound of your greeting,
the child in my womb leaped for joy.*
Luke 1:44

Heartburn, Etc.

I never knew what heartburn was . . . before the third trimester set in. Until now, all those ads for heartburn medication left me feeling good about being able to save money in at least one area of my life! Now I'm trying to remember what those medicines are called.

How many more things can possibly change in this body of mine? I don't think I even know myself anymore. All the energy I've spent during the first 30 years of my life learning how to respond to my body has been trashed! My body hasn't been in such tumult since puberty.

Here's one more example—all these feelings got stirred up by a simple case of after-dinner heartburn. It doesn't take much to make me explosive these days . . .

**Imagine your greatest concern today
puffed up like a marshmallow.
Surround it with the warmth of God's love
and let it melt.**

---

*Grace to you and peace from God our Father
and the Lord Jesus Christ.*
II Corinthians 1:2

Complaining

I feel like a broken record. I'm always complaining about my back hurting and about not being able to sleep. I can't seem to quiet my fears about how everything is going to happen in the delivery room. These worries keep tumbling into my dinner conversations with John, and breakfast conversations, and phone conversations when we call each other at work. I feel badly because I'm sure that listening to all my fear doesn't help John cope with his.

Or maybe it does. If pain loves company, maybe fear does, too. He doesn't talk about his as much, but then there's not much time left after all my spewing. I'm afraid I've saturated him with all my complaining. Will my record be stuck until our baby's birth day? I'll try hard to talk about one other thing tonight besides my pregnancy.

**It's nice to know I have Someone
who never gets tired
of hearing my repeated fear and complaints.**

---

*Trust in him at all times, O people;
pour out your heart before him;
God is a refuge for us.*
Psalm 62:8

Stress

My back and shoulder muscles used to pull together in pain to let me know when I was under too much stress. Suddenly I have a new indicator. Last night my baby stuck a foot or elbow or something sharp into my rib cage, pushed, and wouldn't quit until I sat down, relaxed, and massaged the little point back into the comfort zone!

I realized, then, that when I get tense, my stomach muscles tighten. Now that they house a person with an increasingly strong opinion, who's getting close to outgrowing these quarters, I must stay relaxed for the good of two of us!

Practice some relaxation exercises.

. . . you knit me together in my mother's womb.
Psalm 139:13

Limitations

Wile I try to get everything done before the baby comes, I forget the limitations of my body. All I was thinking about today was that my dog needed a bath. I wanted to check that little item off my list of things to do.

I didn't forget that Tipper hates baths, but I did forget that I can't lift 70 pounds as easily as I used to, especially 70 wiggling, resisting pounds! My body's feeling a little stressed. I hope I didn't damage the baby.

At least I didn't have to lift him back out of the tub. I did have to clean up the whole house after his escape, though.

**Let your respect
for your body's needs and limitations
grow with your size.**

---

*Praise the Lord . . .
he blesses your children within you.*
Psalm 147: 12,13

Flat On My Belly!

I really am losing it! Tonight I was out for a walk and fell flat on my belly. Somehow I misjudged the curb, and, because I had both hands deep in my pockets, I couldn't get them out in time to break the fall.

I was terribly scared I had hurt the baby. I rushed to the doctor, concern taking over my actions instead of my feelings of foolishness. She humored me with an exam and then comforted me with, "Your body is the safest possible place your baby could be." How would I know that? I've never done this before.

It looks like the greatest harm was to my glasses. John knocked them off my face in his flurried attempts to break my fall. I can deal with that.

**Drink an extra glass of water
with a prayer that the fluid around your baby
will continue to provide safety.**

---

*I, the Lord, am its keeper;
every moment I water it.
I guard it night and day so that no one can harm it . . .*
Isaiah 27:3

When My Water Breaks

$\mathcal{I}$'m already starting to worry about what will happen when my water breaks. What if I'm in a restaurant or standing on a friend's plush carpet, or, worse yet, in church! I better start sitting in the back, close to the aisle.

Maybe I should start wearing pads when I go out and carry a bigger purse so I can fit a towel into it! Why haven't I read advice about this in any of my books that discuss enduring the end of pregnancy? I don't even hear other women talk about when and where they were when their water broke. Maybe this event becomes less significant by the time labor and delivery are over.

**Talk about your fears
to someone who has already experienced
this stage of pregnancy.**

---

*When you pass through the waters,
I will be with you . . .*
Isaiah 43:2

Purpose for Baby

My baby has been doing some serious kicking this month! Does that indicate an active child after birth also? If I were to guess at a personality based on the fetal movements, I predict an energetic, gregarious baby will soon be moving around this house.

In the Bible, children were thought to have a stated purpose for life from the moment of conception. Their names subsequently proclaimed that vision and held the meaning of life they proceeded to carry out. I find that to be more than a pleasant idea. I like to think my child already holds the seeds of the meaning he will give to the world. That thought makes the kicks bearable.

**Pray that you can help to nurture
the purpose for which your baby
has been created.**

---

*The children struggled together within her;
and she said,
"If it is to be this way, why do I live?"...*
Genesis 25:22

Belly Patting

$\mathcal{I}$ was just reading suggestions about how to keep people from patting your belly when you're pregnant. They were all ingenious, funny, and bound to be effective, but I had never really thought about trying to make people stop.

Maybe if *strangers* touched me, it would strike me as inappropriate. When friends touch my belly, however, I regard it as a blessing. It doesn't seem like it's me anyway, as much as my baby, who has already taken over that part of me. I can understand, too, that my friends are so amazed they just have to touch to see if it's real. I do the same thing myself.

Think about what touch can communicate.

For thus said the Lord of hosts . . .
Truly, one who touches you
touches the apple of my eye.
Zechariah 2:8

Backache

Tonight the sink and counter are cluttered with dirty dishes. If John doesn't wash them, they will still be there in the morning because this woman's back has had all it's going to take for one day. It hurts so much I can't even make myself do the exercises that are supposed to relieve it! I just want to go to sleep.

This child is already changing my priorities. I still hate to wake up to dirty dishes in the morning. That, however, is no longer the worst thing I can imagine.

**Let go of some of the "shoulds"
in your life.**

---

*Let a little water be brought,
and wash your feet,
and rest yourselves under the tree.*
Genesis 18:4

Supportive Friend

W hat a gift! A friend called tonight as I was struggling to think of something to eat and asked if she could bring supper over and eat with us. I was served at my own table, with no need to dress up or leave a tip! She even washed the dishes.

To top off the treat, she got a video and gave me permission to fall asleep before it was over if I wanted to. What a perfect ending to a wonderful evening—drifting off to sleep in the company of an understanding and happy friend without feeling guilty. She'll never know what a perfect gift she gave me . . . unless she is pregnant herself one day.

**Thank a friend
who has been supportive.**

---

*. . . my needs were supplied
by the friends who came . . .*
II Corinthians 11:9

Reality Shock

A friend came this week to help us get the spare bedroom changed from storage space to a nursery. He helped clean it out, put up a new wall and light, and lay new carpet. Now the reality of our baby is cemented into my being and our house.

The reality has been coming increasingly closer. A long line of validations, from a positive pregnancy test, to hearing the heartbeat, to watching my skin stretch, has given me a growing sense of my impending motherhood. When another person helps to prepare for our baby, though, it all feels even bigger and more real. The thought that this is really happening to me has hit again, a shock of electricity running through me.

**Pour blessings on my helpers, Lord,
as they have blessed me.**

------

*. . . your right hand has supported me;
your help has made me great.*
Psalm 18:35

Balloon

$\mathcal{I}$ watched a man at the park, today, blowing up balloons. I thought, "That's what I feel like! A balloon." As he tied them and let them float to the end of their ribbons, I realized that I lost the analogy at that point. I'm growing farther and farther away from the possibility of floating!

I do feel like a balloon that's being blown up slowly and steadily, but I'm glad there's more than air inside. I wish I were as transparent as a balloon so I could watch everything that's happening in there.

While I sat musing in the park, a balloon slipped off the helium machine and shot into the air. It quickly returned to the earth with a great deal of to-do, more limp than it began. Do I rejoin the analogy there, after I give up what I'm now holding in my ballooned belly . . . ?

Are you feeling more like a lead balloon or one full of helium?

O Lord, you are my God;
I will exalt you, I will praise your name;
for you have done wonderful things,
plans formed of old, faithful and sure.
Isaiah 25:1

Planning for After the Birth

When I was little, I remember that Grandma showed up by my bed in the morning after another sister or brother was born. I remember her scurrying around the kitchen, helping us get dressed and doing the household chores. I remember watching the new baby, too, but my memory picture doesn't have my mother in it at all. She must have been in her room, living the reality of a spent balloon.

John and I talk about wanting to have the first days to ourselves after the baby is born. Should we consider more seriously my mother's offer to come stay with us for a week or two? Does she know something we don't about how much help we'll need? She might know something I don't about a lot of things!

As you plan for your baby's welcome home, don't forget to plan for your needs as well.

Each one helps the other,
saying to one another,
"Take courage!"
Isaiah 41:6

SIDS

Sudden Infant Death Syndrome is such a strange thing. It's especially scary because it kills a seemingly healthy baby without any warning. Even though I don't smoke or use drugs, which are some of the possible contributors to the situation, there's no guarantee that my baby won't die of SIDS. When I think about SIDS, I find myself wishing that the first year of my baby's life, the time of greatest risk, were over before it has even started.

That's no way to live. I don't want to be dominated by the fear of what *could* be. There is no end to possible worries. Sometimes expecting this baby seems to be endless worries, battling inside me with the wish not to worry!

God, preserve my peace.

Do not worry about anything,
but in everything
by prayer and supplication with thanksgiving
let your requests be made known to God.
Philippians 4:6

Multiplied Anxiety

Sometimes, concentrating on my desire not to worry only seems to intensify my jitters. Yesterday I worried about SIDS. Today my anxiety has blossomed to include lots of other fatal diseases, accidents, broken bones, and undesirable personality traits. How does anyone ever live through infancy and childhood? How do *mothers* live through their children's infancies and childhoods?

I want someone to hold me and assure me that everything will be okay, that my baby and I will experience no trauma. I know no one can do that. Life is not predictable nor easy to understand.

**Give stability to my heart, Lord,
especially when I can't quit thinking
about how little control
I have over the future.**

---

*And the peace of God,
which surpasses all understanding,
will guard your hearts
and your minds in Christ Jesus.*
Philippians 4:7

Beautiful

In high school I used to say things like "I'm so fat," just so I could hear my friends say, "Oh no, you're not." Or I'd say, "I wish I were pretty," and hope someone would say, "Well, you are!"

I'd like to think my self-confidence is a little more stable and directed from my inner strength than it was when I was a teenager. Lately, however, I feel like I'm regressing. I don't want to stoop to manipulating compliments from others. It would be nice, though, to hear someone say that I'm beautiful, because I've been changing too fast for my own self-confidence to keep up.

**Listen for God's quiet confidence of love
and imagine it filling you to overflowing.**

*How graceful are your feet in sandals,
O queenly maiden!
Your rounded thighs are like jewels . . .
Your navel is a rounded bowl
that never lacks mixed wine.
Your belly is a heap of wheat,
encircled with lilies.*
Song of Solomon 7:1,2

Power in Naming

*I*f I had known that choosing a name for the baby would so increase the reality of its presence, I would have worked harder at pinning down a name before. I still don't know if it's Jessica or Jonathan bumping around in here, but "Baby J," our new name, already holds more personality than "the baby."

I didn't expect the naming of my baby to be so powerful. Baby J, however, has grown to greater proportions in my heart, in my love, and in my reality. Baby J is a real person who will occupy more than a space inside me. Baby J is mine, different than anything I've ever owned. I love Baby J.

**Give thanks
for the stages your love
has already taken in these months of pregnancy.**

---

*For we know only in part . . .
but when the complete comes,
the partial will come to an end.*
I Corinthians 13:9,10

On Medication

I'm haunted by the fact that I took medication when I was first pregnant, but before I had it confirmed. I knew taking it was a gamble. But I also knew that I could feel better with the medicine. Besides, I thought my chances of becoming pregnant that week were so slim that I decided to take care of myself.

My doctor told me not to worry about it. My friends tell me to forget it. My head informs me that worrying now won't change anything. But I still feel rotten. How could I have been so selfish? I can let go of the guilt for days at a time, but then it creeps back in, playing horror games with my conscience.

**Put an image of a strong,
healthy baby in your mind
to pull up when fears
of the unknown loom heavily within you.**

---

*Can a woman forget her nursing child,
or show no compassion for the child of her womb?*
Isaiah 49:15

Part of Creation

Tonight I want to just lie on the couch, be still, and think about what's happening to me, to my body, to my baby, to this new little world that's being created. Quietness is unusual for this extrovert to long for, but it seems a normal shift that matches the mood of my pregnancy.

The books say my baby is totally formed already, with all the necessary organs to live—even little fingernails and fuzzy hair covering the skin. My baby is working hard to get ready to live out here with me. My body is working hard, too, aiding this preparation while I sit silently, meditating on the mystery of the tiny person being steadily created within me.

**Thank you, God,
for using me to create this life.**

*For the creation waits with eager longing
for the revealing of the children of God.*
Romans 8:19

Mood Swings

Where did that woman come from who waltzed into my house this morning and used my lips to yell at my husband for leaving dirty dishes on the table? She was so irritated when my dog wouldn't quit barking, she tried to kick him with my foot. I was glad, later, that he had gotten out of her way just in time. My husband got out of her way pretty fast, too.

It's scary how quickly she took over my body—unannounced and out of control. I could tell my husband and dog were surprised, too. They didn't see the other woman. They thought I was acting weird. But that wasn't me. I don't want that to be me!

It was me, though. It was part of me. It was, however, only a part of me. Hopefully a temporary imbalance of hormones.

**Accepting the mood swings
of your pregnancy
may help you handle your irrational feelings
better than if you staunchly resist them.**

---

*Set a guard over my mouth,
O Lord; keep watch over the door of my lips.*
Psalm 141:3

Simply Mommy

Today I overheard a four-year-old tell his friend that he has such a good daddy because he married such a good mommy. He didn't care that his mom is a chemist or that his dad has a master's degree in social work. It only mattered that they were good parents, and it was convenient for him that they had chosen to marry each other.

This process of becoming a parent is like working for another degree or changing vocations in midlife. All I have studied and worked to become will have little meaning to my baby. "Mommy" and "Daddy" will be our most important identities as far as our child is concerned, for many years to come.

**God, help me to learn how to be a mommy,
even though I can't be formally trained
or earn a degree for it.**

---

*Trust in the Lord with all your heart,
and do not rely on your own insight.*
Proverbs 3:5

Expert on Motherhood

Isn't it absurd that so many people become parents with so little training? What other job do you know of for which there is such scant preparation or testing? Yes, there are parenting courses and books, but no one is required to learn from them in order to qualify as a parent!

On the other hand, I have been learning how to parent since the day I was born, by feeling, hearing, and experiencing my own parents. I have watched other parents. I know what I like and don't like about the parenting styles I've seen.

In fact, I'm probably an expert on parenting at this point—at least until my baby's birth brings everything into question!

**Write down your hopes and dreams
about the kind of mother you will be
for your baby.**

---

*Happy are those who find wisdom,
and those who get understanding.*
Proverbs 3:13

Friends

When I was a child, our family never lived near our relatives. From the time I left home as a teenager, I have followed that same pattern. I like to visit my family and I miss them, but I've never made decisions about where to live, based on where they are. In fact, I've never given it much thought, until now. Being pregnant, I'm thinking how nice it would be for our child to grow up near grandparents, aunts, uncles, and cousins. When I need childcare, I would prefer to call on my family, rather than using a bought "service" that feels like the big, cold world.

Most of our friends who live near us don't have family nearby either. We have sort of created family for each other—celebrating holidays and personal milestones together, sharing cookies and hot chocolate after playing in the first snowfall of the winter, and connecting by phone when we need someone to listen. I guess my baby can find "family" in friends and neighbors in the same way.

If you think of your friends and neighbors as family, you will broaden and enrich your life.

. . . Better is a neighbor who is nearby than kindred who are far away.
Proverbs 27:10

Risky

*H*aving a baby who grows into a child, who turns into a teenager and then leaves home (or worse yet, won't leave home!), is downright risky! It's not that I have a choice anymore. I grant the choice has been made. I just feel a little out of control . . . well, okay, *a lot* out of control!

Some days I think about how cuddly and dependent on me my baby will be. I imagine her as a sort of possession or hobby. But some days I think about how quickly this baby will become an independent person, unwilling to be controlled. That's when this whole venture seems like a huge risk.

How does your journey into parenthood resemble other risks you've taken?

O my God,
in you I trust;
do not let me be put to shame . . .
Psalm 25:2

Pity Party

I can't stop crying and I don't even want to. I sort of want John to know I'm crying, but I don't know what I'll say if he asks what's wrong. It's just a lot of little things. Nothing went right today.

I waited an hour to see the doctor, and I hadn't taken anything along to do. What a waste of time. The long, slow line at the post office was longer and slower than usual, and I was only there because the new mail carrier is too scared of our dog to deliver our mail. His boss says it's my problem, not his employee's. John and I had an argument about how much money to spend for Christmas. No one won.

One of my friends called to tell me about her awful day. She never asked about my day, and I didn't have the energy to tell her. I only have enough energy to feel sorry for myself. I believe I could cry all day.

Know that you don't have to explain your tears to receive God's comfort.

Let my cry come before you,
O Lord; give me understanding . . .
Psalm 119:169

Anticipation

Tonight neither John nor I could think of what to make for supper when we got home late from work. We checked the phone messages to be sure no one had called to invite us over for dinner (fat chance!) and then went out to eat.

We had a good time, but not nearly as much fun as last month's dinner which we had anticipated for a week. Then we made reservations at our favorite restaurant and invited good friends to meet us there. That restaurant was not nicer than the one we ate at tonight; the food was not better. But the joy of looking forward to a special dinner all week was a bright spark in the middle of my work and otherwise ordinary moments of life.

Anticipating a child is like that, too. When I think about the coming of my baby, it cheers up the drudgery of the routine details of living!

**Enjoy the anticipation
and hope
that's alive in your ordinary life!**

---

*Let your steadfast love,
O Lord, be upon us, even as we hope in you.*
Psalm 33:22

Hands

I use my hands in almost every creative process I undertake (except thinking). When I write, make music, work on crafts, decorate cakes, and clean the house and dishes, I use my hands. I love my hands.

Soon my hands will be busy with a new kind of creativity. They will hold and caress, change tiny clothes and dirty diapers, wash and dry a baby. I'm eager to observe my hands learn how to nurture and create a new space for this child.

Tonight they lie empty and still. They hold my giant belly that has become strangely familiar. They wait for any little movement that will connect them with their jobs to come.

Thank you for my hands,
O God,
and for the way they connect me with life!

Let my prayer be counted as incense before you,
and the lifting up of my hands
as an evening sacrifice.
Psalm 141:2

Womb

I'm jealous of my baby today. I am worn out by the world rushing by, honking and knocking me out of its way. Busyness doesn't interest me enough to try to keep up with it anymore. I wish I had a womb to curl up in, an umbilical cord through which to receive unsolicited nourishment, and protective fluid in which to float with no worries. I would have no knowledge of stress, schedules, or social etiquette, nor would I care.

The womb beautifully symbolizes unconditional love, acceptance, and pure simplicity. No worries exist there about clothes or food or breathing. And to think I have that to give to another person! I am held in awe, as if in the womb of the One who continues to nurture me into the fullness of life.

**Meditate on how it feels
to have been created with a womb.**

---

*. . . it was you who took me from the womb;
you kept me safe on my mother's breast.*
Psalm 22:9

Omnipresent

"Oh yeah, I forgot you're pregnant!"

"I hope you're kidding," I retorted, "father of this child. It's your pregnancy, too!" He wasn't kidding, though. He said that he can be at work for hours or even days without thinking of his impending fatherhood. There's nothing in his schedule that has changed yet, besides going to a few doctor's appointments with me. He still sleeps comfortably through the night and rides his bike, and he isn't trying to decide whether or not to keep his job after the baby is born.

I'm not sure whether I envy or pity him. I guess it depends on which day we're talking about. He's more free, but he's also missing the constant presence of this child and the reminder that his life will soon change. Maybe that change will feel even more drastic to him.

Find a way to remind the father of your child that he's "pregnant," too.

Those who go out weeping,
bearing the seed for sowing,
shall come home with shouts of joy,
carrying their sheaves.
Psalm 126:6

I Can't Wait

I've been pregnant long enough now. It's been fun—well, part of it has been fun, but I'm ready for the next stage now. I want to see my baby. I want to hold her with my arms instead of my weakening stomach muscles. I want to go for a walk, pushing him in a stroller instead of spending an unfamiliar amount of energy going half a mile. I want to eat junk food instead of being constantly vigilant for the brain cells of my developing baby.

What I really want most right now is to be able to sleep on my stomach again!

**What will you miss
about being pregnant?**

*But if we hope for what we do not see,
we wait for it with patience.*
Romans 8:25

Massage, Scratch, and Grow

The elasticity of skin is amazing. I keep thinking my belly has stretched as far as it possibly can, and then it stretches some more! Can it really keep growing like this for two more months?

I find myself absentmindedly massaging the huge expanse, as if it belongs to someone else. I can almost see new cells popping out between the old ones, like a time-lapse film of a flower bud opening. My belly is always itchy, too. I wonder if that's all part of the plan to make sure I take time to touch my baby, even now.

**Enjoy your baby's first home
as you recreate it day by day.**

---

*And Joseph also went up from Galilee . . .
with Mary, his espoused wife,
being great with child.*
Luke 2:4,5 (King James Version)

Walk, Bike, and Diminish

These days I can't imagine my belly growing one day bigger. But an even harder concept to grasp is that it will someday return to its previous position of relative flatness. I fear it won't, but neither do I want to listen to people who tell me that motherhood ensures permanent weight gain.

I'd rather imagine myself as one of those new mothers that everyone exclaims over, a week after they've given birth. They are the ones who look just like they did before pregnancy.

I must admit, though, the percentage of those kind of women is low. I think I'll go buy that baby seat for my bicycle I saw yesterday in the window.

Claim what control you have with your body, and marvel at everything else that happens to it.

. . . says the Lord.
For as the heavens are higher than the earth,
so are my ways higher than your ways . . .
Isaiah 55:8,9

I'm Huge!

People often tell me I haven't gotten that big. When I say I'm due next month they can hardly believe it.

But they don't feel the extra weight when I climb the stairs now. They can't look down from my nose and see that I don't remember, nor do I have an easy way to find out, what shoes I'm wearing. They don't struggle to regain my balance after I stoop to pick things up from the floor. They don't black out from moving too fast. They don't see me in the shower.

I'm huge. I feel like an elephant!

**Don't expect others to understand your needs.
Baby yourself
according to what you know you need.**

---

*. . . I will strengthen you,
I will help you,
I will uphold you with my victorious right hand.*
Isaiah 41:10

Remember the Elephants

So I feel like an elephant—and I look like one—but I'm thankful not to be one. When I think this pregnancy will never end, I remember the elephants who carry their young 18-22 months before giving birth! When I fear the dependency of a baby, especially during its first year, I remember the elephants who nurse their young almost five years before the calf learns to use its own trunk to eat! I will remember that calves are 140-214 pounds at birth, when I feel like I'm carrying a lot of extra weight.

I no longer feel like an elephant! After considering the ways of the elephant, I am more grateful than ever.

**Thank you, God,
for creating me
with a relatively short gestation period
and for a small baby to birth.**

---

*God made
the wild animals of the earth of every kind . . .
And God saw that it was good.*
Genesis 1:25

Remember the Sparrows

*A*s the days wear on and my baby grows more and more out of proportion to the size of the opening from which he or she must eventually emerge, I get increasingly uneasy. That's a calm word for it—uneasy!

Not being an elephant makes me grateful. Then, again, I'm glad I'm not a mother sparrow. She lays two or three sets of eggs every year, probably painlessly, but certainly without the element of joy and love with which I carry this baby. I wouldn't find it nearly as rewarding to watch my baby hatch as to work at this process together, all the way to the end. I'm also glad I don't have to sit in one spot to keep my baby warm and protected!

**Think, with gratefulness,
about the unique ways
in which you have been created.**

---

*So God created . . .
every winged bird of every kind.
And God saw that it was good.*
Genesis 1:21

Made for Relating

*L*ast spring a robin chose our yard as a place to lay her eggs. We were happy she picked the lowest cradle of branches in the weeping cherry tree as the place to build her nest. Then we could easily count the eggs and later watch the baby birds.

I was amazed by how fast they grew. I thought we would have all spring to watch the happy family, but, after the eggs hatched, the nest was abandoned by the whole bunch of them within two weeks!

Sometimes I dread how long this baby will be dependent on me, but I'm certainly glad we'll have longer than two weeks together. I need a lot longer than that to share my values, to gather the wisdom my child will offer, and to experience the simple (or complex) ups and downs of life together.

**Thank you, God,
for creating me with a need to relate
and a way to do it.**

---

*Remember how short my time is . . .
Blessed be the Lord forever.
Amen and Amen.*
Psalm 89:47,52

Against My Nature?

The robin who had a nest in our backyard permitted us to get very close to her without flying away. We walked within two feet of her nest on our way to the gate, many times a day. Our dog lay or barked within a few feet of her, depending on his mood, and she wouldn't budge! That mother's primary job, after the nest was built and the eggs were laid, was to protect them, even though that instinct must have conflicted with another natural instinct—self-preservation.

It makes me wonder how often, as a mother, I will be called upon to protect or love my baby at the expense of my usual way of doing things. Will my pride have to bend to allow me to properly nurture my child? Will I even recognize me when I'm a mother?

**Pray that neither fear nor pride
will stop you from giving what your child needs.**

---

*Look at the birds of the air;
they neither sow nor reap nor gather into barns,
and yet your heavenly Father feeds them.
Are you not of more value than they?*
Matthew 6:26

Off Balance

I wish I could feel a little more balanced in my life. I get irritated with people more than usual. I couldn't agree with my friends about what kind of pizza to order today! I said okay finally to save face, but I boiled inside when I was expected to help pay for "their" pizza. I know I'm being ridiculous, but I can't find my own Stop button. The one I usually push to minimize problems isn't working.

My whole body is off balance. It aches when I make it stand up to wash dishes. Lately, the ache starts when I even *think* about washing dishes! It's my turn to clean the house this week. That irritates me, too. Maybe I should swallow my pride that wishes John would *offer* to do it, and simply ask him to help. It's so frustrating to feel this imbalanced in my spirit and body.

**Begin writing your unspoken feelings
in a journal
to see if they will name themselves.**

---

*In my distress
I cry to the Lord,
that he may answer me.*
Psalm 120:1

239

Embrace Life

I started making a list today of all the things I want to do one more time before the baby is born. I want to go out to a movie with a friend before I have to line up a babysitter in order to do it. I want to eat at Bogart's, my favorite restaurant, where it takes too long to be served, but the atmosphere is so enjoyable that I don't mind. I want to go see my sister without worrying about how someone's going to stay in a car seat for six hours. I want to visit the art museum when I can go at my own pace and stay as long as I want to.

My independence is running out. I want to embrace it enough to last me for a long time! I'm so tired, though. Maybe I'll go out tomorrow night.

Enjoy the freedom
you still have to sleep
whenever you want to.

. . . a time to embrace,
and a time to refrain from embracing.
Ecclesiastes 3:5

Insomnia

Nothing is more disgusting than giving up one last night out with a friend so I can catch up on my sleep, only to find I can't go to sleep! I was undoubtedly exhausted, but I simply couldn't sleep. My baby was ready to wake up and play when the lulling motion of my movement stopped.

I couldn't get comfortable. I couldn't stop thinking of all the things I could be doing instead of lying in bed wide awake. But I couldn't make myself get up either, because I kept thinking of how tired I'd be the next day if I didn't sleep.

I have this eerie feeling that I'm being conditioned for sleep patterns yet to come. That thought will probably keep me awake tonight, too!

Practice deep breathing exercises.

. . . even at night
their minds do not rest . . .
Ecclesiastes 2:23

Sex: What's That?

It's good I became pregnant eight months ago because it could never happen now! I have never felt less sexual in my life. I think I've already turned the corner into motherhood and lost my sense of being a wife in the process. I'm big enough to be a cow, and their sexual practices don't appeal to me at all.

I hope this won't be my permanent state of being. I'm sure my sexual appetite will become normal as my body does, in another month or two, or five. For now, a back rub is the most loving touch I can imagine receiving. I'm glad our commitment is greater than sex.

**Reinforce your love
and receive love
as honestly as you can.**

*I am my beloved's
and my beloved is mine . . .*
Song of Solomon 6:3

Braxton Hicks

I woke up at five o'clock this morning to an unsettling tightness across my abdomen. Half asleep, I readjusted my stomach pillow to ease the tension. The tightness turned into pain, however, and my brain awoke with a start. I was going into labor!

I was paralyzed with a mixture of fear and excitement. It's not time yet! The baby doesn't understand time schedules, though.

I jumped out of bed and started packing. By the time I was dressed, I realized that I hadn't felt any more contractions. Then I remembered that real labor is supposed to start in my back.

Oh well, I'm relieved to know my body is getting ready and that I can still move fast if I have to. I'm glad to have my bag half-packed for the hospital, too.

**If you're hyper-vigilant,
at least be sure you can laugh at yourself.**

---

*. . . my loins are filled with anguish;
pangs have seized me,
like the pangs of a woman in labor . . .*
Isaiah 21:3

Still Balanced?

I'm so disgusted. After riding my bike to work every day for years, John says I can't do it anymore, just because I'm eight months pregnant. He jumped to an incorrect conclusion when he came home and found the mirror on my bike broken. He won't believe me that the bike fell over after I parked it, because he read something about women losing their balance when they're pregnant.

I admit that his caring feels good, but I wasn't ready to give up my favorite transportation yet. How much will I have to give up for this child? I have a feeling this is only the beginning . . .

**Go ahead and grieve
the losses this child already brings.**

---

*The Lord will guide you continually,
and satisfy your needs in parched places . . .*
Isaiah 58:11

Advent

Now that I'm in my last month of pregnancy, I find myself thinking about what Mary may have experienced during her last month of carrying Jesus. I'm thinking that my usual way of preparing for Christmas—baking, eating as much as possible, being with lots of friends, and buying and making gifts without end—is probably as opposite as I can get from that first Advent.

In these final days of my pregnancy, I especially love the silence of night. I want to pay attention to the growth of this little ball of holiness inside me, and that happens most easily when I'm alone.

Rather than roaring through a host of festivities, I will quietly watch the candles burn down.

**Light a candle
and imagine waiting with Mary
for your holy birth.**

*. . . Mary treasured all these words
and pondered them in her heart.*
Luke 2:19

Bed Rest

This is the moment I've dreamed of—to be ordered to bed by the doctor. The only time I can remember spending this much time lying down is when I've been too sick to enjoy it. Now I'm a little uncomfortable, but I feel good enough to read the magazines that have been piling up and to work on the baby announcements between my spontaneous, luxurious naps.

That was two days ago. Today it got old. I want to get up and clean my own house (I never thought I'd say that!) and shop for my own food. I'm losing my patience with pillows and couches. The only thing that ties me down are the heartstrings connected to this tiny heart inside, ready to do anything for my baby.

Make friends with the notion of sacrifice.

. . . the former things shall not be remembered
or come to mind.
But be glad and rejoice forever
in what I am creating . . .
Isaiah 65:17,18

*I*t's rainy outside today, and I'm rainy inside. Everything feels rainy. It's dark and gloomy outside; people scurry from one shelter to the next. I can't hide from my inner rain. It pelts my lack of defense and leaves me with more questions and less answers.

Why did I think I could be a mother? How did I figure a child would fit into my life? Nine months didn't used to be this long. My body is giving out on me. Will it ever be the same as it was before I was pregnant?

I sort of feel like crying, but I don't think I will. The fears feel like they're outside me, like the rain that falls everywhere without discretion. I'm not drastically upset, just quietly gloomy.

**Turn your concept of rain
from gloom
into a substance of nurture.**

---

*I am poured out like water,
and all my bones are out of joint . . .*
Psalm 22:14

Healing Waters

*I*t's still raining outside, but today the rain feels cleansing and healing rather than like an agent of despair. When I think of myself as an earth mother, nurturing the growth of this new life and paying attention to how we're connected to the total creation, I remember I need the rain as much as the earth needs it.

I grow during moments of darkness and quiet because that's when I take the time to be still and receive nourishment. I am able to nurture this new shoot out of the moisture I receive from the healing rain. When it's too wet to go out, I celebrate the coziness of a rainy day.

**Rain is often defined
by your perception of it.**

---

*He does great things and unsearchable,
marvelous things without number.
He gives rain on the earth
and sends waters on the fields . . .*
Job 5:9

Eighth Month Rationality

I suddenly have this bizarre urge to move to a different house in a different part of town. It doesn't seem bizarre to me. I just know it would sound that way to someone else if I said it out loud.

I want to do something new. I want to have the best possible home for my baby. I want everything to be just right.

I do still have some rationality left in me, though. It would be fun to move, but when I'm eight months pregnant is probably not the best time to make a major change.

Maybe I'll channel my enthusiasm for something new into painting the nursery. I've got to have something fresh to tide me over until I have a new baby to take my energy.

**Let your imagination and desires roam,
but check them with a good friend
before acting on them.**

---

*. . . I am the Lord your God,
who teaches you for your own good,
who leads you in the way you should go.*
Isaiah 48:17

Deep Breathing

oday I got to practice the deep breathing exercise I've been learning in my childbirth education classes. I was waiting in the doctor's office an hour past my appointment time again! I got so intensely impatient that my stomach and shoulder muscles contracted and I was afraid of scrunching my baby. So I made myself practice the breathing techniques I'll soon need for labor and delivery.

I felt disrespected by the doctor, who didn't even apologize for wasting my time. It was nice to know, though, that I still had some control over how I responded. Maybe I'll be able to use deep breathing for the rest of my life!

**Love your baby
and yourself enough to relax
and breathe deeply.**

[God] grants peace within your borders . . .
Psalm 147:14

Instant Change

I was thinking recently about last summer's vacation to the Colorado Rocky Mountains. We spent a year planning the trip, and then a six-hour flight and a two-hour drive put us in the snow-covered peaks. As we walked the 20 yards to the cabin, we lost our breath and had to rest before ascending the stairs—slowly. We hadn't anticipated the thinner air at that altitude. We soon rescheduled our hiking plans to give our lungs time to get used to their new limits.

I wonder if having this baby will be like flying to Colorado. One minute we don't have a baby. The next minute we do. When I start sharing my air and my time with this baby, maybe I will be ready to readjust my activity schedule and pace.

**It's hard to know now
how much you will need to readjust.
Imagine a couple of different situations
to see how easily you can live
with various levels of energy.**

---

*. . . we will all be changed, in a moment,
in the twinkling of an eye . . .*
I Corinthians 15:51,52

251

Lower Expectations

Okay, so I will need to slow down after the baby is born. Have I been pushing too many things into the "To Do When the Baby is Sleeping" slot? My pile of magazines to read is growing. When I think of another letter to write, I add it to that future "empty" time. It's not full of anything I know about yet, so it feels empty. That's what maternity leaves are for, right? That's when I relax and catch up on all the details of life I've forgotten during pregnancy.

But what if having this baby leaves me as breathless as flying to the Rockies? Maybe I'd better start planning my landing at home in the same way that I'll plan my next vacation to the mountains—with plenty of time for relaxation and as little expectation to produce as possible.

**Don't assume
you'll have more time
after your baby is born.**

---

*The Lord protects the simple;
when I was brought low,
he saved me.
Return, O my soul, to your rest . . .*
Psalm 116:6,7

Clumsy

I am tired of people telling me to be careful, of people carrying things for me, of people running ahead to open doors for me. Just because I'm going to have a baby doesn't mean I'm totally incapable of taking care of my myself!

So I defiantly grabbed the pie that my mother-in-law had made, as we divided up loads to carry into the house for Thanksgiving dinner. I was being careful, but, in the middle of the front porch steps, my right leg flew out from under me and I landed with an elbow in the pie.

Being pregnant is so humbling.

Pray harder.

Bless our God, O peoples,
let the sound of his praise be heard,
who has kept us among the living,
and has not let our feet slip.
Psalm 66:8,9

Crying Spells

*L*ast night I walked into the room that's supposed to be the nursery and broke down, crying uncontrollably. It still looks like a study and I'm just tired of waiting! There's too much to do before the baby comes. We'll never get it all done on time.

I had no energy to do any cleaning; no energy, even, to quit crying. I had no energy to care about how silly my reasoning, or lack of it, sounded. Walking into my messy kitchen had the same effect on me two days ago, so last night I at least had the sense to stay out of the kitchen!

**Don't waste any energy trying to explain
your bizarre emotions.
Know that they're normal,
though admittedly disconcerting.**

---

*May he grant you your heart's desire,
and fulfill all your plans.*
Psalm 20:4

Nesting

$\mathscr{I}$'ve heard jokes about the nesting instinct that hits women near the end of their pregnancies. I was secretly glad that I had not been overcome by this force that seems to leave its victims helpless to do anything but grab a sweeper and clean furiously for days at a time. It doesn't sound like fun to me!

But now I'm starting to wonder if my crying spells over not having everything perfect and in order are part of that nesting instinct. Even when I don't have energy to work at building the nest, I am frustrated about not getting it built! Maybe it's all part of the same thing. "Nesting" is preparing the way for our growing family. I do want to do that.

What preparations have you made for your baby, whether or not you've called it nesting?

They shall not labor in vain,
or bear children for calamity;
for they shall be offspring blessed by the Lord . . .
Isaiah 65:23

Out of Breath

I feel like an old woman as I trudge up stairs that seem to grow instead of lead to a landing. I don't have enough breath to finish two lines of music with gusto. If I dance with joy, I quickly collapse into the nearest chair, preferably an overstuffed one.

I feel like an old woman, until I remember who's claiming that extra oxygen. And then an excitement wells up inside me that shoots out with wings. I'm young again and running through a field, bursting with the blossoms of spring. I'm on my way to give birth to a more beautiful flower than I can yet imagine!

**Breathe deeply of your dreams
and give your baby some extra oxygen today.**

---

*. . . the mountains and the hills before you
shall burst into song,
and all the trees of the field shall clap their hands.*
Isaiah 55:12

Overwhelmed

It always feels like a major deal to me to schedule a visit to the doctor. I have to figure out the best time to take off work, and then decide what things would be easiest to rearrange when the doctor isn't available in the slot I thought would work best. And then I have to readjust my schedule after every visit because I always have to wait to be seen longer than I expected or think is respectful. Yes, it's definitely been a lot of work every month, and then twice a month, that no one seems to appreciate.

Today she said, "I'll see you next week. You'll come in every week now until your baby is born." It sounded so simple from her end. She's already there. Of course it's easy for her, but I don't have time for this. I have too much to do yet before the baby comes.

**Complain to someone
who can help feel sorry for you
when you feel overwhelmed.**

---

*O Lord, you will hear the desire of the meek;
you will strengthen their heart,
you will incline your ear.*
Psalm 10:17

What's Really Important?

When I am overwhelmed, it helps to get my feelings on paper and also to express them out loud to a friend. How have I handled stress in the past? In school, at the end of a term when I had too much studying to do for the amount of time I had available, I adopted this attitude: "Of what eternal value is it if I make an A or a D on this test?" That usually freed me to take a coffee and doughnut break with my friends!

When I asked myself that question again last night, with all the things I want to do yet before the baby is born, I recognized that my baby's health has more eternal value to me than any other plans. So if I need to see the doctor every week to make sure everything is okay with the baby, there's nothing better I could be doing with my time.

**Test your priorities
by comparing them to their eternal significance.**

---

*. . what does the Lord require of you but to do justice,
and to love kindness,
and to walk humbly with your God?*
Micah 6:8

Who's in the Mirror?

I made the mistake of looking in the mirror when I got up this morning. Whose tired eyes were looking back at me out of that bloated face? How did that nightshirt get so stretched out in the front? And whose huge ankles poked out below it?

I wasn't sure if I should laugh or cry. I sort of did both. It's so much me, and yet not me at all. I've been pregnant forever, and yet this is a totally new experience!

Maybe looking wasn't a mistake. I want to enjoy this state of being as much as I can because it won't last much longer. I wonder if I'll miss being pregnant.

**What can you celebrate
about this day of pregnancy?**

---

*You shall see,
and your heart shall rejoice . . .*
Isaiah 66:14

Enjoy Being Pampered

*I*t's almost comical the way people jump in front of me to open doors, carry my groceries, and give me the most comfortable seat. The bigger I get, the more help I'm offered.

At first I felt somewhat indignant, knowing I could open my own doors and take care of myself just fine. Then I thought about how little of my life I get babied, compared to how much I'll soon be giving to the next generation. I've decided to enjoy every gift that's given as long as it lasts, and to know in my heart that I *could* have done it myself. I think it's more fun for the givers this way, too.

**Soak up the nurturing offered to you,
since you'll be generating it soon enough!**

---

*You, O Lord, will protect us;
you will guard us from this generation forever.*
Psalm 12:7

Is It Labor Yet?

What if I don't recognize labor when it starts? I've heard horror stories of women having their babies in taxicabs or hospital elevators. That would be so awful, and it could happen to anyone—even me! All my carefully laid labor and delivery plans could be worthless if I don't know I'm in labor soon enough.

They say I'll know. They can't describe it exactly, but they assure me that I'll know labor has begun long before my baby appears.

I wish "they" were me. I wish I would know more precisely what to expect. I know it's one step at a time. It just feels like all the scariest steps are suddenly piled up together at the end!

**Relax and listen to your body.
That's how labor will most easily be recognized.**

. . . by paths they have not known I will guide them.
Isaiah 42:16

Labor and Delivery Fears

The bigger I get, the more I think about the small size of my baby's escape route. Something seems backward about this process. Why can't we have labor and delivery first and then go through pregnancy?

Nothing has jolted me out of the peacefulness of pregnancy like that video in our birthing class about what the end will be like! I know it's supposed to be the beginning of life, but right now my fear is blocking my optimism.

God, help me enjoy the present, trusting the future to you.

When a woman is in labor, she has pain . . .
But when her child is born,
she no longer remembers the anguish
because of the joy of having brought a human
being into the world.
John 16:21

My Mother's Replica?

*I*n the early part of my pregnancy, I assumed that I would stay at home and be a full-time mom after the baby was born. As I've thought about it further over the last several months, I am less sure that I really want to do that. But I keep hearing an inner voice that says staying home is the right thing to do because my mother and mother-in-law did that.

Today I saw myself folding diapers the way I remember my mother folding my little brother's diapers. How much of my motherhood will I unconsciously pattern after how I was mothered? Probably most of it, unless I consciously decide differently!

Some of whom my mother was I will replicate with joy. Some I want to change. Change, I am sure, will require more work, more awareness, and decisive action.

Journal about how you want your mothering to be the same or different from your mother's.

When I was a son with my father, tender,
and my mother's favorite,
he taught me . . .
Proverbs 4:3,4

Foundational Memories

9've heard people talk about being guided through meditation to search their memory until they remember the experience of being in their mother's womb and being born. Some talk of the peace of that time; others of the trauma. Both were probably present for mos people

Sometimes I think I would love to crawl back into my mother's womb and be as free-floating and carefree as my baby is now. Today, I feel grateful for the chance to provide a safe environment for a baby. I love being host to this child's beginning memories of being loved. My baby will always have this foundation of peace. After birth I know the Creator will continue this good work.

**Close your eyes
and imagine that God is holding you.
Float aimlessly in a womb
of safety, peace, and love.**

---

*. . . no one can see the kingdom of God
without being born from above.*
John 3:3

Helpless

This morning I had to ask my husband to tie my shoes. It was all I could do to slip them on, and then they were out of my sight and reach. I guess it was funny. John obviously thought it was, but I am frustrated with my increasing limitations. I feel helpless. I'm not supposed to reach things up high. I can't reach things down low! I shouldn't get up fast. I can no longer sit in a stuffed chair if I ever expect to get out of it.

I didn't mind giving up my turn at cleaning with our big old clunky sweeper. I am having a harder time giving up dressing myself! Maybe I should just be glad I can still squeeze my toothbrush into my puffy little face all by myself!

**Know that you are as loved
in your state of helplessness
as much
as your helpless baby will be loved.**

*Know that the Lord is God.
It is he that made us
and we are his . . .*
Psalm 100:3

Episiotomy

All these new words to learn! Who ever wanted to learn the word "episiotomy," or, worse yet, experience the procedure personally? I hate to even read about it. Who wants to sit around thinking about being cut?

Statistics say my chances of being cut to help facilitate birth are fairly high. The hospital where we plan to go has particularly high statistics. When I voiced my fear to our childbirth instructor, she said, "By the time you're ready for that decision to be made, an episiotomy will be the least of your worries." Oh, help. Somehow that wasn't the comfort I was hoping to hear. Maybe I'll go hospital-shopping.

**Choose your battles carefully,
reserving your energy
for what you can control.**

*. . . I will march to battle against it . . .
Or else let it cling to me for protection,
let it make peace with me . . .*
Isaiah 27:4,5

Baby Shower

I was not prepared mentally or emotionally for what happened when I walked into my friend's living room last night. All those people had taken an evening out of their busy schedules to help prepare for and celebrate the coming of my baby!

They had put energy and money into their welcome, too. A table was piled high with brightly and carefully wrapped gifts—all for my baby, whom they were welcoming without having yet met it.

I was completely overwhelmed. Each little sleeper I unwrapped shocked me with the reality of someone who will soon wear it. Every rattle, bottle of baby lotion, and soft blanket drew me closer to the knowledge that someone will soon use them.

I laughed and cried at the same time. I was surrounded by the love of friends and felt quite undeserving.

**Know that you deserve this turn
at being treated like royalty,
whether or not you feel like you do.**

My heart overflows with a goodly theme . . .
Psalm 45:1

Not Mine Alone

Underlying my sense of being loved and taken care of at the baby shower were other feelings that pricked a little. They are hard to put into words, yet they are real in the middle of everyone's welcoming joy. That community of friends, excited with me all at the same time in a party atmosphere, jolted something within me.

For most of my pregnancy, I've enjoyed a cozy aloneness with my baby. It was my secret. I was in charge of feeding our bodies, of trying to maintain a relatively peaceful spirit. Suddenly I'm sharing my baby with everyone. They are all claiming a part in welcoming the life of my baby. My baby has already become more than mine.

**Think about the friends
who are helping
to welcome your baby into the world
and what they will add to the life of your family.**

---

*. . . I have lent him to the Lord;
as long as he lives,
he is given to the Lord.*
I Samuel 1:28

Needing a Community

When I first thought about sharing my child with my friends, I felt like I was opening my hidden treasure box to the world. I imagined becoming vulnerable to any tidal wave that would sweep in to claim my jewel.

When I think about my individual friends, however, and how each has added much joy to my life, I know I want to share my baby with them. My baby will be richer for being connected to many people of differing gifts, talents, and ways of loving. I like to think, too, that my friends will be richer for sharing life with my child.

**Create a photo album
with pictures of your friends
who make up the welcoming party.
Save it to give to your baby.**

------

*. . . may your friends be like the sun
as it rises in its might . . .*
Judges 5:31

$\mathcal{I}$ say, "It could be a month yet!"
John says, "It could be any day."

The issue is this: I want to make a 500-mile trip to attend my family reunion. He wants to stay close to our doctors and the hospitals we know.

I can't blame him. I want to give birth to our baby here, too, but if the baby isn't born this week, I don't want to have missed the party! Our doctor won't take sides. "Traveling this late in pregnancy is always a risk," she says, but she also offers to give us copies of our records to take along.

It's an odd predicament. We've never argued before about whether or not to travel! We have always said in unison, "Let's go!" This baby is already making us work harder at our decisions.

**Calculate the risks,
and then find a way
to enjoy the consequences of your decision.**

---

*All went to their own towns to be registered . . .
While they were there,
the time came for her to deliver her child.*
Luke 2:3,6

Vessel

I visited Betsy in her studio today. She told me she's been doing paintings with a vessel theme, so I went to see her work.

I don't know why she's painting vessels, but as soon as I saw them, I knew that, for me, they are paintings about pregnancy. They are mostly large canvases, up to six feet by nine feet, painted in deep reds and rich blues. The vessels are all in motion, busy, purposeful. They look like I feel.

That's who I am. I'm a vessel, holding life and enhancing my own at the same time. No matter how static I may look to someone who watches me in a Sunday morning pew, I'm busy, moving, with the most important purpose possible. I'm a pregnant vessel, painted with the rich hues of blood and royalty.

Paint your image.

The precious children of Zion,
worth their weight in fine gold—
how they are reckoned as earthen pots,
the work of a potter's hands!
Lamentations 4:2

Flurried

I have two friends who are new mothers. One of them is thoroughly enjoying parenthood. She appears relaxed; her responses to her baby seem to mingle easily with taking care of her own needs.

My other friend lives in a flurry. She pushes her baby carriage around the neighborhood like she needs to break a record.

The first friend is happy to be living out this part of her life dream. The second seems to be caught off-guard, wondering where this baby came from.

I have both friends within me. I can understand both kinds of attitudes and feelings. And I'm glad for both examples. Hopefully, because of them, I can more clearly choose which way I want to live my motherhood. Otherwise I'm likely to succumb to the untamed mood-of-the-day.

**Pray for the strength which,
at this point,
only God knows you will need.**

---

*. . . I will turn the darkness before them into light,
the rough places into level ground . . .*
Isaiah 42:16

Not Ready

We went to visit the hospital tonight. Our doctor thought it would be a good idea for us to become acquainted with where we will go when labor begins and to see the rooms where we'll be after the baby is born. We were supposed to be reassured and comforted, so things will be more familiar when it's our turn.

What it felt like, though, was utter panic! I looked at that room full of babies, some sleeping, some screaming, and there was nothing in me that wanted to take one home. It was so nice to know they all have their own mothers, and it's not my turn to be one yet.

**Pray that you will be ready
when it's your turn to become a mother.**

*. . . The Lord is the everlasting God,
the Creator of the ends of the earth . . .
He gives power to the faint,
and strengthens the powerless.*
Isaiah 40:28,29

Reassurance

After panicking about not being ready to be a mother by the time my baby is born, I asked some of my friends to pray for me. I want to love my baby passionately. I want to long for my baby to wake from her sleep so I can feed her again. I want to cherish my baby the way a mother is supposed to do naturally.

I've had a feeling, though, that I can't generate those responses on my own. Thus, my request for prayer.

My friends thought I was joking. Who ever heard of a mother not overcome with love at the first sight of her baby? I hope my anxiety is a joke. I pray it's a joke. In my heart I know it will be a joke. But I'm still glad they promised to help me pray.

**Prayer can only help,
no matter how silly your feelings might seem.**

*Thus says the Lord who made you,
who formed you in the womb and will help you:
Do not fear . . .*
Isaiah 44:2

C-Section

Cesarean section or C-Section; however you say it, it's downright scary. I know it's a possibility, and I know a lot of babies are born with that procedure, and I'm trying to be an adult about this, but please, God, don't let me have a C-Section. What if I faint from the idea of being cut open and miss the whole birth? What if John faints and I don't have my coach?

A group of us who are pregnant were talking about C-Sections last night, but everyone else seemed so factual. As far as I could tell, I was the only one scared of it. All I can figure out is that they all think it won't happen to them.

On the other hand, I guess it would be easier for the baby. Maybe I'm being selfish.

**Be ready for anything
and then let go.**

---

*Do not fear, for I am with you;
I will bring your offspring from the east,
and from the west I will gather you.*
Isaiah 43:5

Trauma of Birth

Being born must be quite a jolt to a baby. After nine peaceful months of being lulled to sleep by the gurgling sounds of my organs, he will emerge into a world full of people fussing over him. After floating aimlessly in the warmth of amniotic fluid, she will be carried away to make her footprint and to be weighed and measured, and then taken to an unfamiliar part of her mother—my arms. After existing effortlessly, he will need to learn how to use his lungs immediately, and his tongue and lips soon after. She will have to fight her way down a long, narrow canal that squeezes her with a new tension, maybe for hours, and she'll never be able to turn back.

Then again, maybe false labor is not really false. Maybe it is the real thing, but the baby decides not to do it after all!

**When you worry about labor,
pray peace for your baby too.**

---

*Before I formed you in the womb I knew you,
and before you were born,
I consecrated you . . .*
Jeremiah 1:5

Awe

A thrill of excitement ran through me this morning when I read that there may be a galaxy forming 63 billion light years away, 10 times the size of the Milky Way! The reality of it probably won't affect my life in any great way, so it doesn't matter if it's true or not. But the possibility reminds me that God never stops creating. That's a reminder that fills my life and the air I breathe with enchantment.

The thrill resonates especially in me today because I am part of that continuing creation. The baby inside me is at least as big a miracle as another galaxy.

**Let yourself be filled,
figuratively like you are literally,
with the miraculous continuation of creation.**

---

*Say to God,
"How awesome are your deeds . . ."*
Psalm 66:3

Goodbye and Hello

*I*t's almost over. It's almost time to begin. The definition of life lies in my perception of it—whether I focus on the stage that's ending or the one that's about to begin.

As I entered my third decade of life, I was mostly grieving the loss of my 20s. As I finished school, I could hardly complete those final exams in the excitement of moving on. In the joy of marrying, I also knew I'd miss some aspects of my singleness.

Farewells and greetings are both important. Both can be hard and/or scary. Today I'm thankful for both. It's been wonderful to be pregnant . . . well, the good days have been wonderful! I'm also eager to begin face-to-face life with my baby! Life is full and good.

**Give thanks for the ending of pregnancy
and the beginning of your new life
as a mother!**

---

*Which of you desires life,
and covets many days to enjoy good? . . .
seek peace, and pursue it.*
Psalm 34:12,14

Respecting Uniqueness

I've always liked children who have minds of their own, those who don't give the answers they've heard someone else say, but who question until they find their own answers. I've always laughed at the ones who stick out in the Christmas pageant because they aren't staying in line or looking angelic. I've been intrigued by those who sing off-key with vigor and whose joy supercedes worry about how others might perceive them. I was amused to see a two-year-old insistent on wearing a winter coat all afternoon in July and a four-year-old who refused to wear long pants unless she could wear a skirt over them.

Unique individuals fascinate me. They have always, however, been other people's children. I wonder if I'll be able to allow my child some social deviance, and maybe even enjoy it.

**Prepare your ego now for someone
who will be very different
from who you are.**

---

*You desire truth in the inward being . . .
teach me wisdom in my secret heart.*
Psalm 51:6

As in a Mirror

I hear parents say that one of the paradoxes of children is that they are separate personalities, making separate choices from their parents, and, at the same time, they are very much like their parents. I am reportedly going to hear words come out of my child's mouth that I didn't know I use. I will watch my actions being repeated before I believe my child is old enough to observe and imitate me.

Can my baby already detect my moods, ways of handling life, and voice tones. Is my way of living forming my baby, even now? I wonder—do I really want to see myself as clearly as this child is sure to show me?

Prepare your ego to watch yourself mirrored in your child.

Create in me a clean heart, O God,
and put a new and right spirit within me.
Psalm 51:10

Induced Labor

I don't know whether I'm excited or scared. What I thought was going to be a routine checkup turned into a birth announcement. The doctor said she's afraid my baby isn't growing anymore. They need to induce labor tomorrow morning! I wasn't ready for this. I was planning to finish packing my bag next week. And I wanted to have my announcements ready to mail, except for the name and size, before I went in. Oh, there's so much to do yet! Is nine months really over? No, not quite.

I just hope my baby's okay.

There's nothing like pregnancy to help one let go of the illusion of being in control!

Arise, shine; for your light has come, and the glory of the Lord has risen upon you.
Isaiah 60:1

Delivery Day

This is worse than waiting to open Christmas presents while the adults are still eating. Now that I know it's time to give birth, I just want to get to it.

But I'm also caught in the wonder of this timeless moment. It will happen soon. The countdown that will change my life forever has begun. I'm hanging in mid-air, in a magic bubble, looking at how life has been. It's just two of us, visible, leaving the house. The next time I come back, the bubble will have burst into three of us!

Can this really be the day I meet my baby? Delivery Day. I think I'm finally ready. Nothing else is important now.

**Enjoy the magic moments as
"The End"
gives way to "The Beginning . . . "**

---

*. . . you shall see and be radiant;
your heart shall thrill and rejoice . . .*
Isaiah 60:5

Birth

When the doctor casually said he could see a head of dark hair, I wanted to scream. What? You see my baby? No amount of work was too much after that. My baby was almost out . . . and then she was!

Oh, I can't believe this. You're the one who was in there? You're the one we've been waiting so long to meet? You're so tiny and precious. But how did all of this fit inside me? Did you really just come out of me?

I'll never be able to stop looking at you. I knew you would be beautiful, and you are—precious and beautiful.

**You, my baby,
are the most precious gift
I have ever received.**

---

*. . . when he sees his children,
the work of my hands, in his midst,
they . . . will stand in awe of the God of Israel.*
Isaiah 29:23

About the Author

Sandra Drescher-Lehman has twice enjoyed the gift of being a Mom-to-Be. She now devotes most of her time to those two children, along with her husband, John. Drescher-Lehman works part-time at a local public mental health agency as a crisis worker. She also works with children in Christian education and worship at First Mennonite Church in Richmond, Virginia, where she is a member.

Other books by Drescher-Lehman are the companion book, *Meditations for New Moms, Waters of Reflection,* and *Just Between God and Me,* a devotional book for teens.